PRESENTED TO

_____

FROM

_____

ON THE OCCASION OF

_____

DATE

_____

We gratefully acknowledge
the contributions of Emily Cavins,
Lisa Bromschwig, Regina Neville,
and Linda Wandrei in ensuring
that the content of *The Great Adventure
Kids Catholic Bible Chronicles* is consistent
with *The Bible Timeline*® Learning System.

Catholic
Bible Chronicles

70 Bible Stories from Adam to the Apostles

Written by AMY WELBORN

Illustrated by MICHAEL LaVOY

West Chester, Pennsylvania

Nihil obstat: Rev. J. Brian Bransfield, STD
               Censor librorum
               May 3, 2021

Imprimatur: + Most Reverend Nelson J. Pérez, DD
               Archbishop of Philadelphia
               May 10, 2021

Ascension
PO Box 1990
West Chester, PA 19380
1-800-376-0520
ascensionpress.com

Cover design: Rosemary Strohm

Printed in the United States of America
22 23 24 25 6 5 4
ISBN 978-1-950784-71-4

CONTENTS

Introduction

Welcome to *The Great Adventure Kids Catholic Bible Chronicles.*

These stories and their illustrations will lead you into a great adventure that began thousands of years ago with Adam and Eve, the first man and woman, and which continues today through the Church that Jesus himself established.

The Bible is a remarkable book for many reasons but most especially because it tells the story of God's family.

Why the Bible Matters

The Bible is God's gift to humanity. It is the Word of God, inspired by God and written down by human authors. Sometimes referred to as Sacred Scripture, the Bible tells us of God's loving plan for all of his people. By learning the story of salvation, we learn why Jesus came as our Savior— to defeat sin and death and offer all people eternal life with God.

The story of God's family is sometimes called salvation history. It starts with Adam and Eve and reaches through thousands of years to the time when Jesus Christ became man and lived on earth. The story climaxes with Jesus' death and resurrection. When Jesus ascends to heaven 40 days after his resurrection, the story keeps going with the Church, which continues his work on earth right up to the present day. This means we are all a part of this story!

Getting the Big Picture of Salvation History

The books of the Bible are divided into two parts—the Old Testament and the New Testament. The Old Testament is about God's promise, or covenant, with the Jews. The New Testament is about how God kept that promise in Jesus Christ.

Sometimes people think they'll understand the story of God's family if they read the Bible from beginning to end. But the Bible is not really a single book. It is more like a small library of 73 books. These books tell many, many stories about people in many places and times, with different themes and subjects.

The books of the Bible are not organized in story-telling order—they are grouped in categories. So books of history appear together, followed by books of poetry, and then books of prophecy, the Gospels, and a collection of letters to the early Christians. This makes it challenging to follow the storyline if you read the books in order.

To help you understand the greatest story ever told, we have selected 70 Bible stories that tell the story of salvation history from Adam and Eve to Jesus and the Church. If you read these chronicles in order, you will experience the story of salvation history from beginning to end.

Understanding *The Bible Timeline*®

When trying to understand what happened to a group of people over thousands of years, a timeline can help. A few years ago, Ascension introduced *The Bible Timeline*, which divides salvation history into 12 time periods. Each period is like a chapter in salvation history.

To make it easier to remember what occurred during each time period, we assigned each one a color related to significant events:

TIME PERIOD	COLOR
Early World	Turquoise, the color of the earth viewed from space
Patriarchs	Burgundy, representing God's blood covenant with Abraham
Egypt & Exodus	Red, the color of the Red Sea
Desert Wanderings	Tan, the color of the desert
Conquest & Judges	Green, the color of the hills of Canaan
Royal Kingdom	Purple, the color of royalty
Divided Kingdom	Black, representing Israel's darkest period
Exile	Baby Blue, symbolizing Judah "singing the blues" in Babylon
Return	Yellow, symbolizing Judah's return home to brighter days
Maccabean Revolt	Orange, the color of the fire in the lamps in the purified Temple
Messianic Fulfillment	Gold, representing the gifts of the Magi
The Church	White, the color of the spotless Bride of Christ

As you read the 70 stories in the *Catholic Bible Chronicles,* you'll see colored stripes on the pages that match *The Bible Timeline* colors. The stripes should make it easier to follow the "big" story.

If you are interested in seeing a picture of how all of the books of the Bible fit into *The Bible Timeline*, you may like *The Great Adventure Kids Bible Timeline* Chart, which is also available from Ascension.

The Stories

Each of the stories is a retelling designed to capture the essence of what occurred. Each story also features an illustration that represents a key scene. We hope that viewing these illustrations helps you enter the story and imagine what it would have been like to be present as salvation history unfolded.

At the end of every story, you will see a line that tells you where to find the original story in the Bible. That line includes a Bible citation, which looks something like this:

Genesis 11:1

Like all books, the books of the Bible have names. Genesis is the name of the first book of the Old Testament. You can find the names of the other books in your Bible's table of contents.

Every book of the Bible also has chapters, and every chapter has numbered verses.

In the Bible citation above, the number in front of the colon (:) is the chapter number, and the number after it is the verse number. So Genesis 11:1 points you to verse 1 in chapter 11 of Genesis.

What if the line says Genesis 11:1-9? That story starts at the verse you just found: Genesis 11:1. But notice the short dash before the 9. The short dash is a hyphen (-), and the hyphen tells you that the number after it is another verse, where the story ends. So this story starts at verse 1 and keeps going through verse 9.

You might also see a citation that looks like this:

Genesis 7:1–9:17

This one looks complicated, but it isn't really. Notice that the dash after 7:1 is longer than a hyphen. The long dash tells you that the number after it is a chapter number—chapter 9. So this story is also in Genesis. It starts in chapter 7 at verse 1 and keeps going. It goes through the entire chapter and the next one until it reaches chapter 9, where it ends at verse 17.

Think of these Bible citations as signs that point you to where you can find a particular story in the Bible.

The Great Adventure®

Bible stories follow the lives of real people—people like us, who were created to know God and love him but who often, instead, turn away from him and go their own way. This is sin, the disobedience that separates us from God. The Bible stories show us how God pursues us—and has always pursued us—despite our sin, teaching us his ways, inviting us over and over again to turn back to him.

God created the world in love. He led the Israelites out of slavery and guided them to the Promised Land. Ultimately, he sent his Son, Jesus Christ, to bring us back to him by his death on the Cross, which freed us from sin. After Jesus ascended to heaven, God sent his Holy Spirit to guide the Church as it continues his saving work.

When we are baptized, we too become part of his Church. We become part of the story—part of God's family, along with heroes like Abraham, Moses, David, and the Blessed Virgin Mary. Their stories are our own family stories!

The Holy Spirit inspired those who wrote the Bible. As you read the *Catholic Bible Chronicles*, ask the Holy Spirit to help you understand the stories. God always wants to reveal himself to us, and if we ask him to, he will. We pray that this book starts you on your own great adventure!

EARLY WORLD TIME PERIOD

Creation to 2200 BC

The Bible begins when God creates the world. Man is created in God's image. But Adam and Eve, the first man and woman, disobey God, and sin enters the world. Sin and sadness spread, leading to a great flood. Later, there is confusion in the city of Babel as people continue to turn away from God.

God creates
the **heavens** and the **earth**,
along with **man**

In the Beginning ...

Before anything else, before you or your great-great-great-grandparents were born, before your neighborhood or town was built, before the earth, the stars—before the entire universe that lies beyond what even the most powerful telescope can see—before any of that was, before any of it came to be, do you know what there was?

God.

God, who always was and always will be.

God, who was never born and will never die.

God, all-powerful, all-knowing, all-loving.

One God in three Persons, a Trinity of love—Father, Son, and Holy Spirit.

Before earth, sun, or stars, before time, before even space, there was nothing at all—except God.

And God spoke.

"Let there be light."

That's all it took. Out of absolutely nothing, into what had been a formless void, came something. What was it? It was just what God said: light. God saw that the light was good. Creation had begun.

God divided the light from the darkness. He called the light "day" and the darkness "night." And that was the beginning of time.

It was evening, it was morning. It was the first day.

And God spoke. He said, "Let there be a firmament to divide the waters." God had made time when he made the light, and now he created space, too. He called the firmament "heaven."

It was evening, it was morning. It was the second day.

And God spoke again. This time he said, "Let the dry land appear." Through his all-powerful word, the waters gathered and the land formed. God called it the earth and the seas, but this was only a start. He spoke again, and the earth was filled with plants: trees and grasses, fruits and vegetables. Great and small, standing tall or waving quietly in the breeze—God gave plants life. But it wouldn't end there, for God made the plants with seeds, ways to keep growing and making new life over and over.

God saw that it was good.

It was evening, it was morning. It was the third day.

And God spoke. He said, "Let there be lights in the heavens." And there were so many lights! Countless stars twinkling through the vast universe.

Then near the beautiful planet earth, teeming with green plants, God set two special lights. The sun would rule the day, keeping the world warm and helping the plants keep growing. The moon would rule the night, so the world would never know total darkness.

God saw that it was good.

It was evening, it was morning. It was the fourth day.

And God spoke. He said, "Let the waters bring forth living creatures, and let birds fly!" And so the seas and rivers and sky filled with life—huge whales and sharks, slow-moving manatees and playful dolphins, swarms of shimmering sardines, and salmon leaping over the rocks. Tiny hummingbirds found the flowers, red-breasted robins built their nests, and great eagles soared over the mountains God had raised.

God blessed all the fish and the birds. He told them to be fruitful and multiply, to fill up the earth with movement, sound, and new life, again and again.

God saw that it was good.

It was evening, it was morning. It was the fifth day.

And God spoke. He said, "Let the earth bring forth living creatures." And so over the plains, on the hillsides, in the forests, and in sunshine, God made the animals.

There were cattle and all kinds of other creatures that walk on four legs. There were animals that hop, crawl, and creep. Great elephants and tiny ants, quick-as-lightning antelope and slow-moving sloths. God created them all, of every kind, shape, and color.

God saw that it was good.

What a beautiful world God had made! Before he spoke, there was nothing, but look at it now. The all-powerful God spoke, and through that powerful word, all of this living, growing, leaping, shimmering creation came to be. The all-knowing God spoke, and through his word, a creation—ordered, changing and growing in cycles, bodies great and small—came to be. The all-loving God spoke, and through his word, a creation of endless delight and beauty came from nothing.

But was there something missing? Even with such beauty, such variety, such power, the earth and the heavens lacked one thing.

God—all-powerful, all-knowing—God, who is life itself, who gives and shares life—God is also love.

And God said, "Let us make man."

So God made one more creature. A creature different from the rest, but still his own, created by his word.

"Let us make man in our image, after our likeness" was what God said. The rest of God's creation reflects God's wisdom, reason, power, and love as a painting reflects an artist's ideas. But in man, God put something different. In human beings, God made creatures who are like him: who reflect and share God's mind and God's love.

God made creatures who can talk to him. Who are free and can choose to grow and become more like him. Who are made to live in union with him now and forever.

And so God created men and women, creatures who could share in his life. Creatures who could reflect his power, wisdom, and love and help God care for the rest of creation.

God looked at everything he had made, from the heavens to the earth, to the seas and the mountains, from the tiniest cell to the woman and man, and saw that it was all very good.

It was evening, it was morning. It was the sixth day.

The work of creation was finished. God had spoken, and now it was the seventh day. On the seventh day, God rested and blessed that time. The seventh day became the Sabbath, the holy day of rest for God—and for us all.

Based on Genesis 1–2:3.

Creation of Woman and Man

What a beautiful world God created! It was full of life of all kinds, growing and flourishing, the work of God's loving, wise hand. Ocean waves glinted in the sunshine, tigers stretched after their afternoon naps, flowers blossomed, the seasons changed, day moved into night and back again, and rain fell gently from the heavens God made.

In the midst of all this beauty, alongside the creatures who crawled, flew, and walked on four legs, strode another creature. He was like the others in so many ways. He reflected the Creator's wisdom and depended, like all the rest, on the loving Creator for his life and every breath.

But this creature was different from the rest. God had formed him from the dust on the ground and given him life when he breathed into his nostrils. He had made this creature in his own image and likeness. And now this creature walked the earth on two legs, his face turned up to the heavens, his arms outstretched.

This creature was a man, walking in the Garden of Eden, free and able to choose to love, build, hope, reason, and most of all, talk and listen to God. God had breathed life into him. God had given him a soul.

In this beautiful Garden, the man had all he needed to live and be happy. God told him to keep the Garden and protect it. God told him he could eat of all of the trees of the Garden, but one: the Tree of the Knowledge of Good and Evil.

As the man walked in the Garden, God said, "It is not good that the man should be alone." And so God brought the animals to the man. He told the man to name the animals, and the man did. He named all the cattle, the birds and beasts. He saw the furry bears, the fuzzy mice, the scaly iguanas, the strutting peacocks, and he named them all.

They were all beautiful and special in their own ways, but not one of them was like him. Not one of them was made in God's image as well, free and able to create, think, and love.

The man had no companion, no other creature to share in the closeness of life. He lay down to sleep.

While he was asleep, God took one of the man's ribs from his side, and from that rib, he fashioned one more creature: a woman.

The man woke up, saw the woman, and said, with joy, "At last! Bone of my bones and flesh of my flesh!"

God had given the man and woman a great gift: each other. He had created them to be together, in union with each other. And he had created them to be in communion with him. He created them to walk in the Garden together. They would be happy and at peace in the midst of all God's beautiful creation. They would have everything they needed. They would be companions, one flesh, each created for the other and for the glory of God.

Based on Genesis 2:4-25.

A **serpent tempts** Adam and Eve

In the beautiful Garden,
the first woman and man lived happily
and at peace.

They were at peace with each other.

They were at peace with the world
around them.

Most important, they were at peace with
their Creator.

God, loving and kind, had breathed life
into them and formed them. He had
created them in his own image to be free,
intelligent, creative, and loving. He had
given them life in this Garden. Here they
had everything they needed. God knew
exactly what they needed to flourish and

to live in communion with each other
and with him. He knew, and here he
provided it all to them.

God told them that everything in the
Garden was good and was good for them
except for one tree—the Tree of the
Knowledge of Good and Evil. The fruit
of every other tree was available to them,
but not this one. If they ate it, he warned
them, they would die.

Would the man and woman obey God?
Would they trust him? Would they be
content with all he had given them?

Would they listen to him?

Or would they listen to another voice instead?

Among all the creatures in the Garden, there was one more crafty than any other. This was the serpent.

One day, the serpent approached the woman with a question. He asked her if God told her that there was any tree in the Garden whose fruit she shouldn't eat.

The woman answered the serpent, remembering what God had said about the Tree of the Knowledge of Good and Evil, standing in the middle of the Garden. She told the serpent what God had said: If they ate of that fruit, they would die.

"No, you won't," answered the serpent. He told her that they wouldn't die if they ate the fruit, but something else would happen: their eyes would be opened. They would be more like God. They would share in his knowledge. "This," he said, "is what God doesn't want: for you to be more like him."

In this way the serpent tempted the woman. He tempted her to replace trust in God's care with suspicion. He tempted her to think that she could be smarter than God. He tempted her to use her freedom to disobey God, who had created her and knew what was best for her. The serpent tempted the woman to look at all the wonderful gifts that God had given her and misuse them.

The serpent tempted the woman to say no to her loving Creator.

And that is what she did. The woman looked at the fruit, saw how beautiful it was, and decided that whatever it could give her was better than what God had promised. She said yes to the tempter and no to God, who had given her everything.

She wasn't alone, though. The man was at her side. He ate the fruit of this tree as well. The man said no to God too.

Before this, the woman and man had lived together in the lovely Garden with nothing between them. They had not been wearing clothes, but neither do newborn babies. The woman and man had lived like that—newly alive in the world, freshly created by God, innocent and free. They had nothing to hide and no reason to be ashamed in front of each other.

In the moment when they ate the fruit that God had forbidden, all of that changed. Their eyes were opened, and yes, they gained a new type of knowledge, but it didn't bring them happiness. The serpent had lied!

They had reached for the wisdom and power that belong only to God: the power to decide what is real, what is true, what is right, and what is wrong. They had disobeyed. They had decided they knew better than God, and instead of joy, all they knew now—as they fashioned fig leaves to cover themselves—was shame.

Based on Genesis 3:1-7.

Adam and Eve are banned from the Garden

What wonderful gifts God gave our first parents so long ago. He created them in his very own image! He gave them the ability to think, create, choose, and love, so different from the other creatures that must rely on instinct to survive.

He blessed them with life and all they needed to live and be at peace. He gave them the freedom to respond to his love in gratitude and trust.

But the woman and man listened to the serpent's temptation and said yes to that instead.

Now, in the cool of the day, the man and the woman heard God. They heard him walking in the beautiful Garden he had created for them out of love.

And they hid from him. They hid themselves from their Creator, who had fashioned them out of love. For the first time ever, they were ashamed and afraid, and they hid.

God called out to them. "Where are you?" he asked.

The man answered from the trees, still hiding. "I heard you coming," he said, "and I was afraid, so I hid because I was naked."

God responded to the man. "Who told you that you were naked? Have you eaten the fruit of the tree I had forbidden you?"

Yes, the man admitted. This was what he had done. But before he admitted it, he did something else. He pointed at someone else: the woman, his wife, the flesh of his flesh whom he had been overjoyed to meet when he first awakened from his sleep. "She gave me the fruit," he said.

And then the woman spoke up with more blame. "It was the serpent," she said.

What had happened?

What had broken?

Trust, openness, and innocence were gone. The man and woman had once walked freely in the Garden, nothing separating them from each other, nothing separating them from God.

Now they covered themselves out of shame and hid from their loving Creator, each blaming the other for their sin.

When they did what God asked them not to do, the man and woman brought discord and pain into the world. There would now be consequences for what they had done, God said. Sad, tragic consequences.

The serpent would crawl on his belly, and there would be enmity—deep, bad feelings—between his descendants and the woman's.

The woman would suffer pain in childbirth.

There would be tension between the woman and the man.

The man's life would be marked by hard work. The earth would no longer just give him what he needed to live. He would have to toil and sweat to bring it forth. And in the end—for now there would be an end to his earthly life—he would return to the ground, dust to dust.

For our first parents, it was now time to go. It was time to leave the Garden, the place God had made especially for them, the place where, if they had just trusted him, they would have had all they needed to live peacefully and happily.

God sewed them clothes out of animal skins. The woman, named Eve because she was the mother of all living, and Adam, the first man, prepared to leave the Garden, for they could no longer live there. At the gates of the Garden, closed behind them, God placed cherubim with flaming swords to guard the Tree of Life.

Where the woman and the man had been open and trusting with each other before, now they were wary and full of suspicion.

Where they had lived comfortably with the rest of creation, now there was painful hard work and even death.

Most importantly, where there had been perfect communion between them and their Creator, now there was distance and shame.

Was there any hope?

Of course there was. God himself offered this hope for the man and woman when he spoke to the serpent. He told the serpent that there would be enmity between his seed and the woman's seed and that, one day, there would be a human being who would bruise the serpent's head.

God was saying that one day a savior would come. Evil had not won the final battle. Eve had said no to God in this Garden. But in another quiet place, at another time, another woman, named Mary, would say yes to God and become the mother of the Savior.

In the Garden of Eden, a man said no to the Father's will. But in another garden, called Gethsemane, Mary's son, the Word through whom God had created all of this, would say yes to the Father's will. And his yes would lead us all, all the children of these first parents, back to the beautiful place that God meant for us from the beginning.

Based on Genesis 3:8-24.

Forty days
of rain **flood**
the **earth**

Outside the Garden now,
Adam and Eve toiled for their food, worked hard to live, and watched as sin and sadness spread. The conflict and distrust that came with their no to God's goodness entered the lives of their children, too. Their son Cain grew so jealous of his brother Abel that he killed him one day in great anger.

That's the way sin is. It keeps spreading until we turn to God and seek his goodness again.

Eventually, sin spread throughout the entire earth. This earth, created by our loving God, was filled not with love, beauty, and peace but with all sorts of wickedness instead. The evil was so great that the Lord was sorry. The sinfulness grieved the Lord so much that he said it was time to begin again.

There was one good man on the earth, though. And his name was Noah.

The Lord spoke to Noah and told him of what he was going to do. He told Noah that it was time for the earth to be renewed and that God would bring this new beginning through Noah and his family.

God would send a great flood to destroy the sinfulness that had spread through the world. But Noah and his family would be saved from the waters, he said. How? Noah was going to build a boat.

God told Noah how to build this special boat, called an ark, and told him to take his family aboard with him: his wife, his sons Shem, Ham, and Japheth, and their wives. And of course, God told him to take animals and birds along!

Noah was to gather the creatures in pairs. There would be a female and male of every kind. Large and small, creeping, walking, and flying, the animals entered the great wooden ark that Noah and his family had made, exactly as God had told them.

And then the rains came. It rained and rained. Waters rushed from the sky and covered the entire earth. Hour after hour, day after day, the rain fell—for forty days and forty nights.

Then the rain stopped, but the earth was still covered with water. After a time, the ark came to rest on the edge of a great mountain, called Ararat, that peaked out of the floodwaters. The rain had stopped, but what would Noah, his family, and all the animals do now?

They could not swim to find land, and they certainly couldn't send the elephants, horses, and dogs out into the deep waters. But one sort of creature could still help—the birds!

So Noah sent a beautiful shiny black raven out one of the windows of the ark. The raven flew around and around, looking for a place to land, but he couldn't find any. Day by day, the waters went down a little more. So Noah sent out a dove, the kind of bird that coos gently in the trees. But the dove returned to the ark too, because it couldn't find a place to land. The waters kept going down, but Noah still couldn't see any dry land.

After a week, Noah sent the dove out again, and that evening the dove returned to him holding a freshly plucked olive leaf in its beak. Noah knew now that somewhere new life was growing on the earth. After seven more days, he sent the dove out again, and this time, the dove didn't return. Noah knew the dove had found a place to rest at last: a home.

In time, Noah looked out and saw, at last, dry land. God had saved them from the floodwaters, and with the Lord's help, he and his family would fill the world with life again. God told them to be brave and go out, to be fruitful and multiply.

Noah and his family were grateful to God, and so, thankful, they prayed. Noah built an altar and offered sacrifice.

In answer to Noah's prayer, God made a promise.

The promise God made with Noah is called a covenant. It wasn't just with Noah himself but with his whole family and all who would come after. God promised that he would never destroy the earth with a flood again, and that he would help all the living creatures be fruitful, multiply, and fill the earth.

God's covenants always come with a sign. The sign of God's covenant with Noah was something we can still see today: a rainbow. God told Noah that a rainbow would be the everlasting sign of his love and protection for his creatures, man and beast.

Floodwaters of different kinds still threaten us sometimes. Danger may surround us. But that danger will never overtake us or destroy us, because God gives us the ark of his Church to save us—and the waters of Baptism to wash us clean.

Based on Genesis 6:1–9:17.

Tower at Babel abandoned

Noah's family grew and grew.

His sons had sons and daughters, and over time, more and more descendants were born, grew up, and created even more families.

Some of these families traveled east and made a home on the plain of Shinar. There, they decided to make bricks, and this is how they did it: They took dirt from the earth, mixed it with water, poured the mixture into wooden forms, let it harden, and then put the forms in ovens. Baking the bricks made them hard and sturdy, like stones. The people could stack the bricks on top of one another and spread a thick material like tar between them so the bricks would not fall. Now they could build walls and tall buildings.

Their leader was Nimrod, Noah's great-grandson. Nimrod was a mighty hunter and a powerful warrior, known and feared throughout the land. He built many cities to show his strength.

The people of Babel wanted their city to be very great. In the city they would build a tower so tall that it reached the heavens. The tower they wanted to make was not as tall as buildings you find in a city today, but it still reached very high—higher than any tower built before. Any people who could build a structure like that in those days would show the world that they thought they were important and powerful.

At this time, all the people spoke the same simple language, and as they talked, they made their plans.

"Let us make a name for ourselves," they said. And they started to build, brick by brick, the city with its tower that would reach to the heavens.

What did they want, and why? Like their first parents and ours, they wanted to be like God. They were reaching for the heavens—not so they could be with God and dwell with him as his grateful creatures, but so they could *be* gods, without God.

God saw what the people were doing. He looked down and saw the tower and heard the people talking and making their plans.

"This is only the beginning," God said. He saw that the people were busy building up power, looking at the world as their own to use and control. They weren't thinking about him or caring for one another. They weren't grateful. God had indeed given human beings dominion over the earth he had made. He had given this responsibility to Adam and Eve and to Noah and his children. But what he gave them was the job of caring for creation and shaping it so that it helped others and reflected God's love and care. He didn't give them free will so they could show off and be proud. He didn't give them the ability to think and create so they could build up their own power. He didn't give human beings the big, beautiful, interesting world so that they could just turn around and forget the One who had created it.

And so God came down and confused the people, so that their words didn't make sense and they couldn't understand each other anymore. And because they couldn't understand each other, they couldn't make their plans. They couldn't build their walls and their buildings and their high tower. They couldn't keep grabbing power for themselves.

God scattered the people throughout
the earth. They abandoned the city,
and the place came to be called Babel.

God confused the people because
they had turned away from him.
But centuries later, in an upper room
in the city of Jerusalem, God moved
among the people again at Pentecost,
uniting them and giving them the gift
of the Holy Spirit so that all his children,
everywhere, could understand his
words of love and hope.

Based on Genesis 11:1-9.

PATRIARCHS TIME PERIOD

2200 BC to 1800 BC

Abraham, Isaac, Jacob, and Jacob's
twelve sons are the fathers, or patriarchs,
of ancient Israel. The stories of this
period begin with the call of Abraham
and end with the family of Jacob, who
is also called Israel, settling in Egypt.

God calls Abram

Years passed. Families grew.

Men, women, and children tended livestock, gathered plants for food, settled on the land, and began to build.

In these days, hundreds and hundreds of years before Jesus was born, many people settled in an area called the Fertile Crescent. In what we now call the Middle East, where the countries of Iraq, Iran, Turkey, and Syria are today, two great rivers flowed: the Tigris and the Euphrates. They did not flow close together, but they flowed in the same direction. The waters of these rivers made the land good for growing, for giving and supporting life. Near the Euphrates River was a city called Ur.

Great civilizations began in this Fertile Crescent. Cities grew there, cities with names we still know today: Nineveh and Babylon. Kingdoms were built, writing was developed, art and music were created.

And it was here that God called a man named Abram to follow him.

Abram was seventy-five years old when he heard the Lord's voice. He was married to Sarai, but they had never had any children. Abram was from that city of Ur, near the Euphrates, but had moved with his family to Haran, further northwest. He and Sarai had moved with his father, Terah, and Abram's brother's son—his nephew Lot.

In these days, some people moved often. They owned and cared for great flocks of sheep and goats that gave them milk as well as fur and meat. In this dry land, the flocks of animals could not stay in one place for long. They would eat all the vegetation in one place and have to go find more. The rains would stop in one area, and the whole big family of men, women, children, and animals would have to keep wandering, to find a new place that would give them what they needed to live.

Abram and his family lived in a place and time when human beings had again forgotten their Creator and closed their hearts to the one, true God. Some worshipped idols instead, little carved figures they made with their hands. Others worshipped the lights that shone from the heavens and the forces that moved through their lives on earth.

But Abram, living amid the sacrifices to idols and arms raised to the sun and moon rather than the One who made them all, heard God's voice.

"Go," he heard the Lord say. "Leave your country, leave your father's house and go to a land that I will show you."

God made promises to Abram. He told him, "I will make of you a great nation. I will bless you and make your name great. By you all the families of the earth shall bless themselves."

Abram didn't have to listen. He didn't have to follow. He could have remained in the place he was used to, safe with the ways and the people he knew, guiding his flocks along familiar roads. But Abram listened to the Lord and followed his voice.

Abram trusted God. He didn't know where he was going. He couldn't be sure where God was leading him. Some of what God told him might not have even made sense to him.

God promised him that he would make a great nation of Abram. When we think of nations, we think of governments and boundaries on maps. When Abram heard God promise that he would make a great nation of him, he heard something different. He heard the promise of fatherhood. From Abram, God said, would come a people joined by faith and kinship. Abram would be a father. Abram would be a patriarch of many!

But how could this be? Abram and Sarai were already elderly. They had no children at all—not a single one.

No, it might not have made sense to Abram. It might have been very hard to understand how God could work through one man and his family to bless the whole world, but that was part of God's promise, too.

Abram had no idea what was in the future or how any of this would come to pass, but he did know this: he knew God's care, and he trusted in it. He had faith.

And so with that faith and deep trust in the one, true God, Abram set forth from what he knew for the unseen, faraway land promised by the Lord: a land called Canaan.

Based on Genesis 12:1-4.

A mysterious **priest** blesses **Abram**

Why did God call Abram
to journey to the land of Canaan?
Why did the people of the world need
to be blessed, and why by Abram
and his family?

When we remember Creation, the
Garden of Eden and all that our first
parents had been promised and what
they lost through their disobedience,
we might see the answer. It's not that
complicated.

God had not given up on us!

Yes, creation was broken. The people
had scattered. Even after the new
beginning of the Flood, discord had
entered the world again. Human beings
fought and wandered far from God's love.

But that is not what God had created
us or any of this world for. In the
beginning, he had looked out on every
bit of creation and declared it to be
good. Like an artist, what he had created
reflected his mind: his love, his wisdom,
truth, and beauty. And he had fashioned
a special creature—man and woman—
made in his very own image, to care for
creation and share his life forever.

To bring us back to him, to heal creation,
to forgive the sins of his children, to
open the gates of paradise once again—

no, God had not forgotten. God would not leave us orphaned, alone with our proud "no." He would give us another chance to use our freedom the way he had intended.

And it would begin with Abram's act of faith and trust. It would begin with one man's yes.

So Abram and his family set forth. They started the long walk south from Haran to the land of Canaan, the Promised Land. And Abram built altars to the Lord where he and his kin could offer thanks: one in a place called Shechem and another in Hebron.

Of course, the journey was not along deserted roads in desolate, empty lands. Other people had settled in these lands, and in time they came into conflict with Abram and his family. Once, several kings waged battles against them, taking Lot and others prisoner, and Abram set forth, fought those kings, and won Lot's freedom.

When Abram returned, it was time, as it always is, to give thanks to God for his help and his blessing. But it wasn't Abram who built the altar or offered sacrifice this time. It was another priest, who was also a king. His name was Melchizedek.

Melchizedek is mysterious. In those times, men were usually identified by their families. They didn't have last names the way we do, so they were known as "the son of" a father or related to others in some way. Even though Melchizedek was very important— he was not only a priest but also a king—his parents are never named, and we never learn anything more about Melchizedek, including how long he lived or when he died.

But we do know this: He came to see Abram after Abram's victory over the other kings. And he came not simply to congratulate him but to bless him.

Usually animals were offered in sacrifice, but Melchizedek didn't bring animals. He brought bread and wine. And he blessed Abram: "Blessed be Abram by God most high, maker of heaven and earth!" He thanked God for delivering his enemies into Abram's hands, and Abram gave Melchizedek a tenth part of everything he had.

It would be a long journey back to communion with the Lord, but here was a beginning. Melchizedek was king of Salem, the place that became the great holy city of Jerusalem, with the name that means "peace." This king of a city that reminds us of the peace

God wants to share with us was also a priest—one who stands between heaven and earth, interceding and praying for us. There would be other priests from among God's people, but Melchizedek would always be special. He was not of the Levite tribe that the regular priests of Israel came from. His priesthood was so great that Abram, the patriarch and father of God's people, shared a tenth of his goods with him in gratitude.

That journey back to communion with the Lord would reach its fulfillment in the one High Priest greater than any other: Jesus. In that same city of Jerusalem, Jesus, one with no human father and the one whom death could not hold in its grip, offered bread and wine and blessed it, and it became his body and blood. That body and blood was offered then, on a hill in that city of Jerusalem, bringing peace to the broken creation, gathering the wandering children of God.

"You are a priest forever according to the order of Melchizedek" (Psalm 110:4).

Based on Genesis 14:18-20.

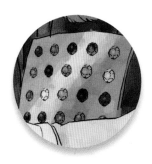

God promises Abraham many descendants

Abram traveled a very long way.

It was a journey of about a thousand miles. He took his wife Sarai and the rest of his family and their flocks of sheep and goats. They traveled along the caravan and trading routes of the Fertile Crescent and then journeyed south to the land God had promised him, the land of Canaan.

Trusting in God, listening to God, Abram and his family had walked. He had fought enemies, rescued his captured nephew Lot, and offered prayers and sacrifices along the way. The king and priest Melchizedek of Salem had met him, blessed him, and offered prayers with bread and wine.

Faithful Abram continued to listen and follow God. God had promised him this land, and here he was in the land of Canaan. God had also promised him many descendants and among them kings ruling over a people who would bring blessing back into the world.

Now it was time for God to deepen his relationship with Abram. After the Flood, God had made a special promise with Noah, a promise called a covenant. He had given the rainbow as a sign of that covenant of faithfulness. It was time for God to make a covenant with Abram and give him a sign, too.

"Don't be afraid," the Lord said to Abram. "I am your shield."

Abram trusted that what the Lord told him was true, but he still had a question. For he and his wife Sarai still had no children. Who would his descendants be?

For the answer, God took him outside and showed him the stars in the sky, scattered, twinkling, too many to count, even too many to see.

"Look," God said. "Number the stars. So shall your descendants be." And Abram's trust in God's promise deepened.

Abram had another question. This one was about the land. Yes, he and his family were in Canaan, but it was not theirs yet as God had promised. How was this to be?

For the answer, God first gave Abram a task. He told him to gather animals: a three-year-old female cow, female goat, and ram and also a turtledove and a pigeon. Abram did so. Then he prepared the animals for sacrifice and laid them on the ground.

The sun set past the distant hills. Night came, and Abram fell into a deep sleep. The darkness was heavy and surrounded him. God spoke to Abram. He told him what would be coming to Abram's descendants: that they would wander and live in a land that was not theirs, and they would be enslaved and oppressed for hundreds of years. But that would not be the end of the story. God told Abram that the people would be freed, and those who oppressed them would be judged. As for Abram himself, he would die in peace.

In these ancient days, before writing was common, when people traveled from place to place, how would you make an agreement, firm and sure? You would use signs, symbols, and gestures, and these would all have great importance and weight. You would give your word, make a promise, offer a gift or a sacrifice, and share a meal with others. These signs and words would be solemn and sacred. One of the ways that people commonly made an agreement was through sacrificed animals. "If I break this agreement," they were saying, "may what happened to these animals happen to me."

In the depth of that dark night, on the dry ground, lay the sacrificed animals. Abram remained there, resting, listening, present to the Lord. In the darkness, light and smoke appeared: a pot pouring forth smoke and a flaming torch passed between the animal parts on the ground, between these signs of life and death. Here the Lord made his covenant with Abram, promising him the land—all the land that surrounded him, from Egypt to the Euphrates River.

God made a big promise and deep covenant with Abram. He promised him great and seemingly impossible things: Through Abram kings would be born, the whole world would be blessed, and the land of Canaan would belong to his descendants. And most impossible of all at that moment, there would be children and grandchildren. Abram continued to trust, and God responded, confirming his covenant promise in a most solemn way that Abram would understand.

The sign of God's covenant with Noah was a rainbow. His covenant with Abram and Abram's descendants would have a sign as well, and that sign is called circumcision, a sign that all the male descendants of Abram would bear.

The covenant brought Abram closer to the Lord. His life was changing and being transformed, and as a sign of that change, of the deep relationship between God and his people, God told him he was also changing his name. Abram became Abraham, and his wife Sarai became Sarah. Again, God assured Abraham that he would be the father of many nations—for that was what his new name meant.

What a beautiful promise and sacred covenant. The world cried out for blessing and peace, and through this covenant, light glimmered in the darkness of human sadness. Perhaps creation, broken and hurt, had hope of healing? God had promised. God would be faithful.

Abraham was grateful. He worshipped. He trusted in God's promise. But he still couldn't help but wonder, and he even couldn't help but laugh as he wondered. He was almost one hundred years old. Sarah was ninety.

Children? Grandchildren? A multitude of nations? As numerous as the stars in the sky? Could this really be true?

Based on Genesis 15:1-21 and 17:1-11.

A **wicked city** is **destroyed**

Abraham was sitting at the door of his tent in the heat of the day when three strangers appeared. For ancient peoples, to be hospitable and welcome the stranger was a sacred obligation. As people traveled, they depended on the generosity of others along the way for food and shelter. You offered help to the traveler today knowing that next week it might be you on the road, needing a place to stay and a bite to eat along the way.

So when Abraham saw the three men, he offered them food and gave them water so they might wash their feet. He rushed into the tent to tell Sarah, who fixed a fine meal for the strangers, making cakes and preparing meat from a young calf.

As the visitors ate, they asked Abraham where Sarah was. He told them she was in the tent. They had some news, they said: they would be back in the spring, and by that time, Sarah would have borne a son.

Sarah, listening behind the doorway to the tent, heard this, and she laughed. She was over ninety years old! A child at her age? How could this happen?

Sodom was a city not far from where Abraham had settled. As Abraham showed the visitors the way to Sodom, the Lord revealed news to him. Sodom was a place of great wickedness. Justice would soon be coming to Sodom, a justice that cried out for the destruction of that wickedness.

Abraham considered what the Lord was saying about Sodom. He asked God, "Will you indeed destroy the righteous with the wicked?" What, he wondered, if there were fifty good people in the city. Would God spare it?

The Lord said yes, he would spare the city for fifty good people.

Abraham admitted that he was nothing but dust and ashes in comparison with the wisdom of God, but he still wondered. What if there were forty-five righteous people there? Or thirty? Twenty? Ten? Humbly, in prayer, Abraham asked the Lord, "Suppose ten good people are found there?" Would God still destroy the city?

"No," the Lord answered. "For the sake of ten I will not destroy it."

As Abraham humbly but persistently prayed for the people of Sodom, his visitors continued on their way. They reached the city and found Lot, who like his uncle Abraham welcomed them and offered them food and shelter, which they accepted.

The men of Sodom, however, were not so welcoming. They heard about the visitors. They gathered outside Lot's house and demanded that he send the travelers outside so they could abuse and hurt them. Lot refused, but the men of Sodom grew violent and angry and tried to break the door down. Lot went out and tried to reason with them, but they grew angrier still. At last, the visitors pulled Lot inside, and a great light blinded the mob outside. The angry men groped about, sightless, and stumbled away.

The visitors told Lot to gather his family and leave Sodom right away, for now, indeed, God would destroy it. The Lord had promised to save it if even a few good people remained. But there weren't even ten righteous people in the city, for no one had come to help Lot protect his visitors. It was time for Lot and his family to leave.

Lot gathered his wife and daughters and set out. He called to the men engaged to be married to his daughters to come too, but they thought he was joking and stayed behind. The visitors who had warned him of the coming destruction urged him on and told him to flee for his life.

"Don't look back," they warned. "Or else you will be consumed."

And so Lot and his family fled. They were running, racing through the valley, away from Sodom to a city called Zoar. Behind them fire and brimstone—hot, burning gases—burned down. Think of what would happen if a meteor fell. Think of the destruction of a volcano, earthquakes, and lightning. It was frightening and terrifying. Of course you would want to get as far away as you could, run as quickly as possible to safety. But wouldn't you be curious, too? Wouldn't you want to see what was happening behind you?

"Don't look back," the visitors had warned.

But Lot's wife couldn't resist. She stopped and turned around and put her eyes on what lay behind her rather than staying focused on what lay ahead. And there she was, as the visitors said, consumed. She would stay in that place forever, a pillar of salt.

Based on Genesis 18–19:29.

Abraham is asked to sacrifice his son

The Lord had promised Abraham and Sarah a child of their very own—and here he was, at last.

In their old age, Sarah conceived and bore Abraham a son, and they named him Isaac. Isaac means "laughter" because Sarah had laughed when she was told she would have a son. Faithful and trusting in God, Abraham could now see the fruit of God's promise, this living and breathing child in his arms. Here was the beginning of the great nations, the first of the descendants who would be as numerous as the stars in the sky.

Isaac grew older. One day, when he was still a young boy, God spoke to his father Abraham. God called to him and told him to leave the place where they were living and take Isaac to Moriah, where there was a great mountain at a distance of many days' journey.

But why? What was the reason for this journey? God did not hide anything from Abraham. He told him he was to take Isaac, go up the mountain, and offer his son—his only son, whom he loved— as a sacrifice.

Abraham rose in the morning. He got one of his donkeys and two servants. He called Isaac, he cut wood, and they set out.

They traveled for several days. On the third day of the journey, Abraham could see Moriah at a distance, and there he told the servants to stay with the donkey. He took the pieces of wood he had cut and laid them on Isaac's back. Abraham himself carried the knife he would need as well as a torch of fire to burn the offering to the Lord.

On they walked. Isaac carried the wood, Abraham the fire. Isaac asked his father, wondering, "Father, we have the fire. We have the wood. But where is the lamb for the burnt offering?"

"God will provide," Abraham answered.

Up on the mountain, Abraham built an altar.

He laid the wood on the stones.

And in obedience to God, who had fulfilled every promise he had made, he bound his son Isaac and laid him atop the wood on the altar of sacrifice. This was the son whom he loved, the son whose life was precious to him, the son of his old age whom God had given to him as the first of a great nation, born to bring blessing to the world.

Why would God ask him to sacrifice his son? It was a great mystery, so very hard to understand. But what Abraham did understand was that he had every reason to trust God and have faith in him. He had no reason to turn and say no. God had been faithful to him. God would, as he had told Isaac, provide.

And he did. Just when Abraham was ready to make the sacrifice, the angel of the Lord called his name from heaven. "Abraham!" he called. "Abraham!"

Abraham answered, "Here am I."

The angel told him not to lay a hand on his son.

It was clear that Abraham's faith was deep and strong, the angel said, clear that Abraham feared God. He would not even spare his longed-for son.

With that, Abraham looked up and saw that, indeed, God had provided. Nearby, in a thicket of bushes, a ram had been caught by the horns and was trapped there. Abraham immediately cut the ram free and offered it to God on the altar he had built there on the mountain.

As the offering to the Lord rose to heaven, the angel called out to Abraham once again with a message from the Lord. Because Abraham had withheld nothing from God, not even his son, he would indeed be blessed. Not only would Abraham's descendants be as many as the stars in the sky, they would be like the sand on the seashore. Who could even begin to count that? From the patriarch Abraham and his son Isaac a great nation would grow, which would have victory over their enemies. All the world would find blessing and light through them, because of Abraham's faith and trust.

Hundreds of years later, not far from this spot, God's only begotten Son would also carry wood on his back. Later, as Jesus' disciples remembered and shared what happened in Jerusalem in those days, they noticed something familiar. They remembered Abraham's faith and his trust in God. They remembered his well-loved son bearing the wood of sacrifice on his back. They understood, even though so much remained a mystery in the heart of God, that indeed, out of the willingness of the Father to sacrifice his Son, all of the world would indeed find blessing.

Based on Genesis 22.

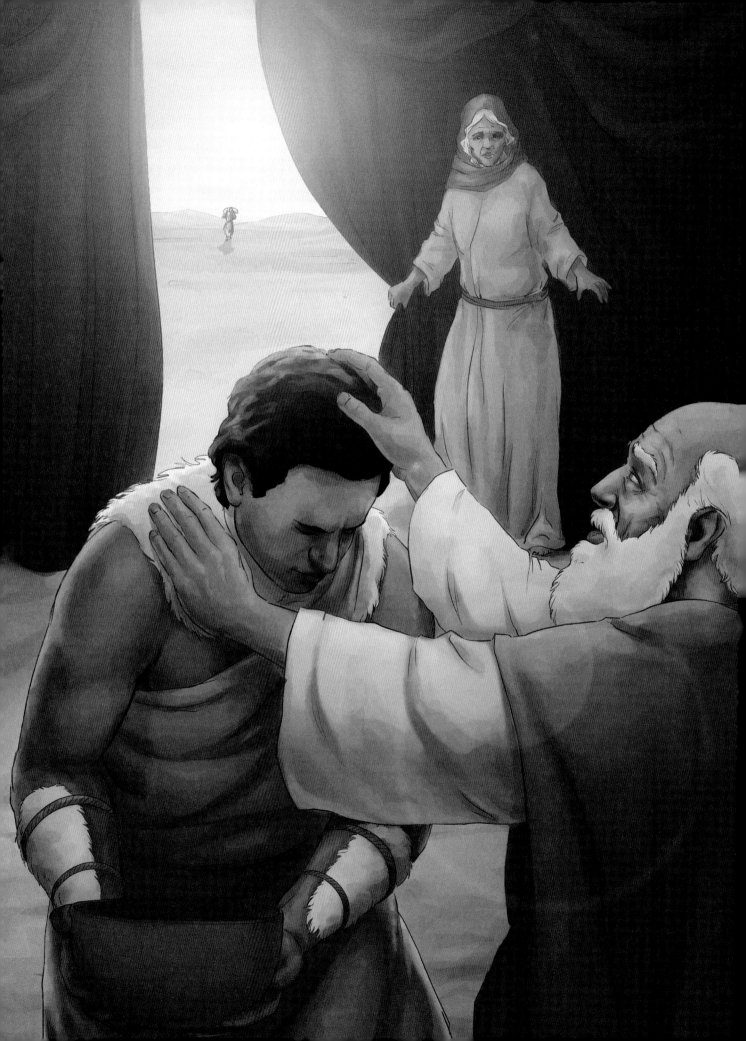

Jacob steals his brother's blessing

The boy Isaac grew to be a man, and it was time for him to marry. Abraham didn't want his son to marry someone from Canaan who might worship false gods. But he didn't want Isaac to return to Haran himself, either— Abraham was afraid he might never come back if he did!

So Abraham sent his servant back to Haran with the important job of finding a wife for Isaac. When the servant reached Haran, he prayed for a sign. He prayed that if he approached a well and asked a woman for water, and if that woman offered to water his camels too, the woman would be the wife God intended for Isaac.

Sure enough, as he approached the well, he had just this exchange with a young woman. Her name was Rebekah, and as it turned out, she was even part of Abraham's big family group. The servant had prayed and listened, and God had answered his prayers.

Rebekah traveled to Canaan, where she and Isaac were married. In time, God gave Isaac and Rebekah children: two at once, as Rebekah was carrying twins!

It was hard for Rebekah, for the twins struggled inside her almost from the very beginning. She prayed for help, and the Lord told her that two nations were struggling within her. He also told her that one day, the older child would serve the younger, which was the opposite of what anyone at that time would expect.

The babies were finally born. The skin of the firstborn boy was reddish, and he was covered with thick hair. He was named Esau. Minutes later, his twin brother, Jacob, was born. Jacob was holding his brother's heel, as if he had been trying to hold Esau back!

In these days, the firstborn son had a very special role in the family. When his father died, he would inherit most of the property and take his father's place, becoming the leader of the family. This special role was called the birthright of the firstborn son. Since Esau was born first, he would become the head of the family one day when Isaac died.

But it didn't work out that way.

Jacob and Esau grew from babyhood to boyhood to manhood. Jacob was quieter and worked among the tents. He was his mother's favorite. Esau was his father's favorite, and he spent his time hunting, away from the settlement.

Once, Esau returned hungry from hunting, and Jacob was cooking a stew of lentils. Esau begged Jacob for some of the food. Jacob said he'd give him some, but only if Esau gave him something in return. Jacob would give him some stew if Esau would give him his birthright. Not lend it, not share it, but hand it over forever so that Jacob would have all the rights of the oldest son.

Esau said, "I'm about to die. What good is my birthright to me right now?" And so he agreed and swore that, yes, Jacob could have the birthright.

Years later, when Isaac was very old and close to the end of his life, he called Esau to him. It was time for him to give his oldest son his blessing. This blessing was a public sign that Esau was, indeed, the firstborn heir with all of those rights. The words that a person said in the blessing were not just words, either. They were sacred and could not be taken back. This was a special, solemn moment.

So Isaac told Esau to prepare. He told him to go out hunting and get the meat Isaac liked best, and then return and fix it for his father, and Isaac would give him the blessing.

Rebekah overheard and quickly called to Jacob. She told him to go get two young goats that she would prepare just the way Isaac liked. Isaac could not see very well, so she thought he could easily be tricked into thinking Jacob was actually Esau. Then Jacob would get Isaac's blessing. But Jacob wasn't so sure. He argued that surely his father would touch him and feel his skin, which was smooth, not hairy like Esau's.

So Rebekah told Jacob to put the skins of a baby goat on his arms, and Isaac would think he was touching Esau, and Jacob would even smell like his brother, the hunter of animals.

Rebekah prepared the meal, and Jacob, disguised, took it to his father. Isaac wondered, because the voice was Jacob's, but he touched his hairy arms and decided it was, indeed, Esau. And so he gave his son his blessing. He prayed that the land would bear great fruit and that other people and nations would serve him and bow down to him. And Isaac prayed that his son's brothers would also bow down to him. "Blessed be everyone who blesses you!" he said, echoing God's covenant with Abraham.

Soon after, Esau came in from hunting, ready to prepare food for his father. Isaac grew afraid and wondered who it was who had come to him before, who had received his blessing. They realized it had been Jacob, and in agony, Esau cried out, "Bless me, also, Father! Do you not have a blessing for me?"

But the words of blessing were a solemn thing and couldn't be given twice. Isaac couldn't just take back the blessing and hand it to Esau.

Esau vowed he would kill Jacob for tricking him first and then tricking their father. And so Jacob fled Canaan. Afraid of his brother's rage, he traveled back to his mother's homeland to live with her brother Laban. The struggle that had begun in their mother's womb continued.

Based on Genesis 27.

Jacob wrestles with God

Jacob held his family birthright.
He had his father's special blessing. But he'd gained all of that through trickery and lying, and so here he was, far from the tents of his home.

There in the lands northeast of Canaan, he saw a well surrounded by sheep. He asked the shepherds where they were from. "Haran," they answered. Haran—the place from which God had called his grandfather Abraham so many years before, the place where his mother Rebekah had come from. Jacob, in a way, had arrived at another home.

Family was nearby, too. The shepherds pointed out a beautiful young woman whose name was Rachel—and she was even a cousin of his! Her father was Laban, Rebekah's brother.

Jacob fell in love with Rachel and agreed to work for her father for seven years in exchange for her hand. At the end of those seven years, which seemed like just a few days to Jacob because he loved Rachel so much, it was time for a wedding!

In those times, weddings were feasts celebrated over many days, but the women were usually dressed under so many layers and veils you could not even see their faces during the celebration. And so it was with Jacob's wedding. The day after the celebration, Jacob discovered that it was his turn to be tricked. For Laban had not given him Rachel, whom Jacob loved, but her older sister, Leah. Enraged, Jacob asked Laban why he had played this trick on him. Laban just told him that in their country, it wasn't the custom to give the younger daughter in marriage before the older one. But, Laban added, if Jacob would work for seven more years—since in this culture, men often were married to more than one woman at a time—well, then, he could have Rachel for a wife, too. So Jacob did.

Over the years, Rachel and Leah had many children. The oldest of Leah and Jacob's sons was Reuben. The youngest two, of Rachel and Jacob, were Joseph and then Benjamin. Jacob had twelve sons in all, and over time, he worked hard, prospered, and grew very rich. He became so wealthy that Laban and his sons became jealous. Once again, Jacob felt his life was in danger, and it was time to leave.

Perhaps now, since so much time had passed, Esau might have forgiven him? Could Jacob take his huge family, his many flocks of sheep and goats, his camels and other riches, and return to Canaan?

And so they set out on the long journey. As they neared the land of Canaan, Jacob sent a message to his brother, telling him that he was coming. Messengers returned with the news that Esau would certainly come out and meet him—with four hundred men with him.

This news made Jacob fearful. This sounded like an army. Was Esau coming to fight him?

And so Jacob prayed. He told God that he knew he was unworthy of all the kindness the Lord had shown him. He shared his fears, not only about his own life but about the lives of his wives and children. He recalled the promise and the blessing God had made through his grandfather Abraham and his father Isaac: that God would make their descendants as numerous as the stars in the sky.

After he prayed, he sent his servants to meet Esau with flocks of livestock as gifts, hoping that if Esau was still angry, this would calm him. In the night, he took his wives, children, and servants and sent them across the river. Left alone, with everyone on the other side of the waters, preparing to meet his brother whom he had wronged so long ago, Jacob had a mysterious encounter with a stranger.

It was a kind of a battle. All night long, until the break of day, Jacob and the stranger wrestled. The stranger could not beat Jacob, and at one point, he touched Jacob's thigh and put it out of joint. As day was breaking, Jacob said to him, "I will not let you go until you bless me." The stranger asked him his name, Jacob told him, and the stranger said that he would now have a new name. No longer Jacob, he would be called Israel, "for you have striven with God and with men and have prevailed."

Jacob asked the stranger his name, but the stranger just responded with another question, asking why he wanted to know. And then the stranger blessed Jacob. And as Jacob limped away to meet his brother, he gave the place of his struggle a name: Peniel. "For I have seen God face-to-face, but lived."

And now it was time to meet Esau. Jacob looked and saw his brother coming with hundreds of others. He approached, bowing, close to the ground.

But Jacob had nothing to fear. For Esau ran toward him, not in anger but in joy. Weeping, they embraced. Jacob offered Esau some of his great wealth as a gift, as a sign of sorrow for what he had done to him, but Esau refused at first, saying he had enough of his own possessions. Jacob insisted, though, wanting to share because, as he told his brother Esau, in this moment of forgiveness, seeing his face was like seeing the face of God.

Jacob had tricked and strived to get God's blessing, but he didn't need to. What he discovered, there on the night before he returned home, was that God's blessing would come to him as he humbled himself, asked for mercy, and remembered the covenant God had made with his fathers. And now blessed, he would know God's mercy and see God's face in the place where each of us can recognize him: that place of forgiveness, mercy, and reconciliation where love, not anger, reigns.

Based on Genesis 32:22-31.

Joseph is sold into slavery by his brothers

Joseph was the favorite son of Jacob, or Israel. Joseph was second from the youngest, and he and his younger brother, Benjamin, were the sons of Rachel, the wife Israel loved best. Israel favored Joseph so much that he gave him a beautiful, special coat: a long robe with sleeves.

Joseph's older brothers didn't think much of this. They were already jealous of Joseph, and Israel's gift made them angry. When Joseph started telling them about his dreams, they grew angrier still.

For Joseph had a gift. He experienced prophetic dreams, and he was able to understand what these dreams were telling him about the present and the future.

When he was seventeen years old, Joseph told his brothers about one of these dreams. In it, they were all binding sheaves of wheat in a field, when all of a sudden, Joseph's sheaf stood up by itself and all of his brother's sheaves bowed down to his.

That wasn't all. Later, Joseph told his already enraged brothers about yet another dream—that the sun, the moon, and eleven stars were all bowing down to him, Joseph. This time, his father Israel was listening, too, and he scolded him. What a ridiculous dream, that in this time, when the older members of a family were the most honored, one of the youngest would imagine all the others bowing down to him!

Israel's family was very large, and he had grown very wealthy, with countless flocks to take care of. His sons cared for the flocks, and to do so, they would lead them far away from the family's tents, seeking food and water for the sheep and goats. They were often gone for days at a time.

One day, Israel called Joseph to him with a mission. His brothers had taken the flocks to Shechem, and Israel told Joseph to go find them, make sure they were safe and all was well, and report back.

Joseph set out and eventually found his brothers near a place called Dothan. They saw him coming from a distance, their least favorite brother. "Here comes the dreamer," they said, and they decided that here, far away from home, was the perfect place to do something terrible and not be found out: they would kill Joseph. They'd tell their father that a wild animal had eaten him. "We shall see what will become of his dreams," they said.

But Reuben, the oldest son, stopped them. It was wrong to shed blood. He suggested instead that they simply throw him into a pit when he got to them—and Reuben planned to rescue him then and get him back to Israel.

Joseph arrived. They tossed him into a dry hole in the ground, too deep for him to escape, and they sat down to eat a meal. While they were eating, a caravan of foreigners approached them through the wilderness. The brother named Judah had an idea. He pointed out that killing Joseph wouldn't bring them any profit and might hurt them. Why not sell him to these traders? They would get Joseph out of their lives, but they wouldn't have blood on their hands. They wouldn't be guilty of murder, at least.

And so, for twenty pieces of silver, they sold their brother to the traders, and off Joseph went to Egypt.

But what to tell their father? A lie, of course.

The beautiful robe with sleeves that Israel had given Joseph had been left behind. The brothers killed a goat, dipped the robe in the blood, and returned to Israel, showing him the robe. What else was Israel to think but that his favorite son had been killed? Israel grieved in the way that people did then: he tore his own robes and wore sackcloth instead, and he mourned for many days. No one could comfort him in his sorrow. Israel was grieved that he would never see his beloved son again.

There was no way for Israel to know that his sons had lied to him. There was no way for him to know that down in Egypt, far away, Joseph was now a slave in the household of a man named Potiphar, an officer of Pharaoh, the leader of the great kingdom of Egypt.

Joseph had been betrayed and humiliated. He had been left for dead and, his brothers hoped, forgotten. But down in Egypt, Joseph had survived. The dreamer lived.

Based on Genesis 37.

Joseph saves his family and Egypt

Crops had failed,
plants were withering and dying, and animals became thin. It was a famine time.

Many were suffering throughout the world, but there was one land where people had enough to eat. In Egypt, the storehouses were full because of one man: Joseph.

Yes, Joseph, who had been tossed into a pit and then sold into servitude by his very own brothers. Taken to Egypt far from his home in Canaan, rejected and abandoned, Joseph the dreamer would save the lives of many.

Potiphar, an important man in the pharaoh's household, had purchased Joseph from the traders. Joseph worked hard and rose to a position of responsibility. But he got into trouble when Potiphar's wife made up stories about him, and he was thrown into prison.

In prison with Joseph were two of the pharaoh's servants, a baker and a butler. Both of them told Joseph about their strange dreams, and Joseph interpreted them correctly. Sometime later, Joseph was still in prison, but the butler had been released when the pharaoh himself started having strange dreams. The butler told Pharaoh he knew someone who could help.

In the pharaoh's dreams, seven fat cows came out of the Nile River, followed by seven skinny cows that ate the fat ones. In another dream, seven good ears of grain were swallowed up by seven withered ears.

Joseph, guided by God, quickly saw that the two dreams meant the same thing: seven years of plenty would be followed by seven years of famine. Impressed, the pharaoh appointed Joseph to be in charge of preparing for those years of hardship.

And the lean times did indeed come, not only for the Egyptians but for those living in Canaan as well, including Joseph's brothers and his father, Jacob.

Jacob heard about the stores of grain in Egypt. He sent all of his sons except Benjamin to purchase grain. Once they reached Egypt, of course they didn't recognize Joseph, but he knew them and wanted to help them. But first he wanted to know if they were sorry for what they had done to him. He wanted to know if they had changed. Would they once again abandon a brother for gain? Joseph decided to see.

He said he would give them grain to take back, but one of them must remain in Egypt. He said this would show that they were honest men and not spies. The rest could travel back to Canaan, but they would have to bring their youngest brother with them when they returned to Egypt.

Joseph's brothers talked among themselves. They remembered what they'd done to Joseph and agreed that this must be a punishment for that terrible betrayal. They were speaking in their own language and didn't think Joseph could understand them, but he did. He could hear that they were sorry for what they had done to him all those years before.

And so he sent them on their way with their sacks of grain, leaving their brother Simeon behind. The brothers returned to Canaan, opened their sacks and found not only the grain but also the money they had paid for it, which Joseph had secretly put there. Now the brothers were very upset, for they thought they might have sold Simeon into slavery without realizing it.

Jacob mourned for two lost sons, convinced that he would never see Simeon again, and he refused to let the others return to Egypt with Benjamin. He would not lose a third son because of these brothers.

But the famine continued. Eventually the grain they brought from Egypt ran out. The brothers needed to go back to Egypt to replenish their stores, but Jacob would not let them take Benjamin. Yet it was the only way, the brothers argued—the only way to get more grain and get Simeon back. Finally Jacob relented, and the brothers returned to Egypt.

Now Joseph saw his little brother Benjamin for the first time in so many years. He asked about their father and heard he was still alive. Overcome, Joseph had to find a quiet place to be by himself to weep, but still he did not reveal who he was.

The next day he sent them back to Canaan, but this time he hid a silver cup in Benjamin's sack. Soon after the brothers left, Joseph sent his servants to accuse them of stealing the cup, which of course they found in Benjamin's sack.

The brothers were taken back to Joseph. Joseph insisted that they leave Benjamin in Egypt, since the cup was found in his sack. But Judah begged him to keep Judah instead, to save the life of their father. He told Joseph how dear Benjamin was to their father, and if they returned without him, Jacob would surely die of grief. "I'll stay as a slave instead," Judah offered. "Let Benjamin go back to our father."

Now Joseph couldn't keep his secret any longer. He sent everyone else out of the room and told his brothers the truth. "I am your brother Joseph, whom you sold into slavery!"

On hearing all of this, Joseph's brothers were amazed, but they were also scared. Joseph had great power. He had authority. They had done a terrible thing to him, and now they were afraid. Surely Joseph would find a way to even the score?

But no. Joseph had been faithful to God all along. No matter what trouble he had found himself in, he had always used the gifts God gave him for good. Joseph understood what his brothers feared. He told them that even though they had meant to harm him, God had used what they did for good—to save the lives of many people.

"Go back," Joseph told them, "get our father, and return here. Bring everyone here to Egypt to live!"

Imagine Jacob's joy when his sons returned with such good news. His people would be able to live in a place with plenty to eat, protected and safe. And best of all, his son Joseph was alive!

Based on Genesis 42–46:4, 49:1, and 49:8-10.

EGYPT & EXODUS TIME PERIOD

1800 BC to 1446 BC

The third biblical period begins with Jacob (Israel) and his family living in the land of Egypt, where a new pharaoh has made them slaves. After a series of plagues, Pharaoh frees the Israelites, Moses parts the Red Sea, and God reveals the Ten Commandments.

New **Pharaoh** enslaves the **Israelites**

All of Joseph's brothers moved to Egypt.

There were twelve in all including Joseph. They brought their father, Jacob, with them together with their wives and their children, seventy people in all, and all their flocks.

Hundreds of years passed, and generations were born and died. Israel, Joseph, and all Jacob's sons died, but their children had children and grandchildren, too. The people of Israel were prospering in Egypt.

Eventually, a new pharaoh came to power in Egypt, and this king didn't honor the promise made in Joseph's day, when the old pharaoh had invited his family to live there. The new pharaoh was bothered by all these children of Israel. There were so many of them—too many for him. This new pharaoh was afraid that the children of Israel, now called the Hebrew people, would join Egypt's enemies and bring him down.

So this new pharaoh made the Hebrews work very hard. He set them to build great cities and labor in the fields. But even so, more and more children of Israel were born.

Finally, the pharaoh issued terrible, deadly orders. He told all the midwives—women who helped other women give birth—to kill the sons of the Hebrews when they were born. The midwives could let the girls live, but the boys were to be killed at birth.

The midwives feared the Lord and wanted to do right, so they disobeyed the pharaoh and let the boy babies live. They told the pharaoh that the Hebrew women were so strong that they managed to have their babies before the midwives could even arrive on the scene!

But the pharaoh wouldn't give up. He told all the people of Egypt—not just the midwives—to kill all the newborn male children of the people of Israel. Let the daughters live, he said, but throw the boy babies into the Nile River. He wanted to make sure that when the Hebrew girls grew up, they would only have Egyptian men to marry.

Working the people of Israel as slaves was one way to weaken them. Killing the boy babies was another way.

One Hebrew mother thought of a plan to protect her baby son. She hid him at her home for as long as she could, but of course, babies grow and learn to move around and make noise. After three months, this mother made a basket for her son, placed him in it, and set it floating on the Nile River. It was like a little ark, giving safety on the waters.

The baby's big sister stood nearby and watched his basket float on the river, to see who would find and save him.

A young woman came to the river that day with her servants to bathe in the cool, clean water. She was the daughter of the pharaoh himself.

She saw the basket, sent her servants to get it, and peered inside. There was a baby, crying. She could see right away that the baby was one of the Hebrew children, for he bore the sign of the covenant that God had given to Abraham. The boy's sister, standing nearby, offered to help.

"Should I get one of the Hebrew women to take care of this child?" she asked.

The pharaoh's daughter agreed, and so the boy's sister went and found the perfect person to raise the boy—his very own mother, of course!

"Take this child," said pharaoh's daughter, not knowing any of this, "and take care of him." She would even pay Moses' mother for the work of raising her own son.

When he was old enough, the child was brought to pharaoh's daughter and raised in her royal home. She gave him a name, too. She said, "I drew him out of the water"—and so she named him Moses.

Once again, God had brought good out of human evil. The pharaoh sought

to destroy God's people dwelling and prospering in Egypt. But God and his goodness can never be stopped. Out of this evil, God worked good. He rescued and raised up a leader who would bring his people out of slavery, back to the Promised Land at last.

Based on Exodus 1:8–2:10.

Moses asks Pharaoh to let his people go

Moses was tending flocks of sheep and goats in a land called Midian when he saw something very strange: a burning bush. But as Moses got closer, he could see that while flames leapt from the bush, it wasn't actually being consumed by the fire.

But why was Moses on this mountain in this place, so far from Egypt?

After he had grown up in the pharaoh's palace, Moses' life had taken a turn. One day he had seen an Egyptian beating a Hebrew man. In a rage, taking matters of justice into his own hands, Moses killed that Egyptian. To escape punishment,

Moses traveled to Midian, far away from Egypt. There he met and married a woman named Zipporah and was put in charge of her father's flocks.

So here he was on Mount Horeb when God called his name from the burning bush.

"Moses! Moses!"

Moses responded, "Here am I."

The Lord then told Moses to stay where he was and remove his sandals. "You are standing on holy ground," he told him. When we come close to the loving, all-powerful God who created us and helps us live, we come just as we are. We go to the Lord, trusting in him, not taking with us the things of this world that we use to hide us, protect us, or make us bigger and stronger. We are humble in God's presence. We are willing to make ourselves small and open—like Adam and Eve before their Fall—in the face of his great goodness and love.

So Moses removed his sandals. And there, out of that burning bush, God told Moses who it was who spoke:

"I am the God of your father, the God of Abraham, the God of Isaac, and the God of Jacob."

Moses hid his face, for he was afraid.

God told Moses that he'd heard the cries of his people and it was time for them to be freed, to be led out of slavery.

Who would lead them? Moses!

Moses, humble before the Lord, listening, still had a lot to say about this. He had questions. He had concerns. He wasn't afraid to bring all of this honestly to the Lord.

First, he insisted that he wasn't worthy. God responded that he would be with him. It would be the Lord who acted and who would protect. Moses had another argument. If he went to the people and

gave this message, they'd ask for the name of the God who was sending him.

The Lord's answer came:

"I AM WHO I AM."

Our names reveal something about us: maybe where we're from or our family background. God's name tells us that he, unlike anything else in the universe, doesn't need any other force or being to come into existence. Nothing causes God, nothing gives birth to God or creates God. God is.

But that wasn't all. God reminded Moses of the history of his people, from Abraham to the present oppression in Egypt. Tell this story, God said to Moses. Remind them of who they are and who I am and what I have promised!

"What is in your hand?" God asked him. Moses told him that it was a rod.

"Throw the rod on the ground."

Moses did, and the rod turned into a snake.

"Put your hand into your robe," God told Moses. Moses did, and when he took out his hand, it was diseased with leprosy. God told him to put his hand back into his robe, and when he took it out this time, it was clean and healed.

God told Moses that if the people doubted, he should show them these two signs. And if that still didn't convince them, he should take water from the Nile, pour it on the ground, and it would turn to blood.

Moses wasn't done discussing this. He still wasn't sure of himself at all. He told God that he wasn't a good speaker. How could he present this case to the king of Egypt? God answered that he, God, was the creator of speech and mouths. Moses could trust him and go. But Moses still wasn't sure! He begged God to send someone else. Please. Anyone else!

God relented. He told Moses that Moses was still the one chosen to lead, but he could take Aaron, his brother, to speak for him.

So Moses took his family and returned to Egypt. There, he and Aaron approached Pharaoh and asked him to release the people—just for three days, to go into the wilderness to meet and worship their God.

Pharaoh would hear none of it. Why should he? He had never heard of this god, he didn't know about him, he certainly didn't worship him. He wouldn't agree to the request, as he didn't want to lose his slaves' labor for even a short time. In fact, the idea made him so angry that he decided to punish the people of Israel.

One of the main jobs of the people of Israel in Egypt was building, and for this they used bricks made of mud and straw and then baked. Now, instead of having all their supplies provided, the people of Israel were made to gather their own straw, making their labor all the more difficult.

The people weren't grateful to Moses. In fact, they were angry because they were suffering even more now. They complained, and Moses prayed, asking the Lord why he'd done this.

And God answered Moses' prayer. He reminded him once again who he was and what he had promised. And he told him to get ready, for he was about to act.

Based on Exodus 3:1–6:30.

Egypt endures nine **plagues**

God created a beautiful, good world. From nothing, the one whose name is I AM poured out that life and created an amazing universe.

But human beings had turned from this generous Creator and gone their own way. Human beings had put their faith in themselves and the work of their own hands, worshipping idols of every kind instead. Men and women had given in to the tempter and brought pride, suffering, and sin into the world.

But God would never forget his beloved creation, the creatures made in his image and likeness. How could he? So God had made a covenant with Abraham, a promise to protect and love and teach the people who would help him bring blessing into the world again.

Those people, the children of Israel, were now suffering and enslaved. They were living far from the land God had given them. Up there on Mount Horeb, from the heart of a burning bush, God revealed himself to Moses, told him his name, and reminded him who he was: the all-powerful, one God. He gave

Moses a mission: to work with him to deliver his sons and daughters into freedom and flourishing in the land he had promised.

So now, with Pharaoh determined to keep the people of Israel enslaved, bound in a land of idols, God would act. He would show Pharaoh and all the Egyptians, even the children of Israel who might have forgotten him, the truth and the power of the one, true God.

The Lord told Moses and his brother Aaron to go to Pharaoh as he was walking by the banks of the Nile River in the morning. The Nile provided all of Egypt, from south to north, with water for drinking and washing, and its great floods every year watered their crops. The Nile meant life.

Moses lifted his rod and struck the river—and God turned the waters of the Nile, where countless Hebrew baby boys had died, to blood. The Egyptians' source of life became a sign of death. But still the Pharaoh's heart was hard, and he would not let the people of Israel go.

Seven days passed, like the week of Creation. Moses returned to Pharaoh and said, "The Lord says, 'Let my people go, so that they may serve me.'" But Pharaoh refused, and now God told Aaron to lift the rod over all the waters of the land. He did—and this time frogs emerged,

covered the land, and then died, leaving their rotting, smelly bodies everywhere.

But still Pharaoh refused.

Now Aaron held out his rod and struck the dust of the earth. Tiny, pesty gnats appeared, covering people and animals, biting and making them itch.

Pharaoh's heart stayed hard, though, and he wouldn't listen.

Flies came next. Aaron raised his rod and swarms of flies entered everyone's home, and the land was ruined.

Now Pharaoh seemed to give up. He told Moses the people could offer sacrifice to their God, but they had to stay nearby.

But Moses knew that his people would be in danger unless they could offer their sacrifices far from the Egyptians. So he went back to Pharaoh time and time again, telling him to let his people go. He told Pharaoh of God's power over the idols and forces that the Egyptians honored and of God's power over life and death. And God sent more plagues, which killed the Egyptians' livestock but not the livestock that belonged to Moses' people. And he sent a plague of boils, or sores, that covered the bodies of both man and beast.

But Pharaoh's heart remained hard. Moses reminded him that God had given him plenty of chances. Pharaoh was still alive, still had earthly authority. Even now he could let God's people go. But he wouldn't, and this time hail fell from the heavens—hail that beat down plants and destroyed all the crops.

Once more, Pharaoh agreed to let God's people go. Moses said that as they left, he would raise his rod to heaven and the thunder and hail would stop. He did so, and it stopped. And just like that, Pharaoh changed his mind and kept them in Egypt.

Now God sent locusts over the land. Locusts are insects that eat every blade of grass, every stalk of wheat in their path. They flew over the land and descended in great clouds, and whatever the hail had left, the locusts ate. There wasn't a bit of green left in the land of Egypt.

Back and forth Pharaoh had gone. Over and over God had shown his power. God had shown that the things of this world, even the most powerful, were created by him. Pharaoh would get angry and then grow afraid and relent, but then his heart would grow hard again, and again he refused to let the people go.

Now it was time for darkness.

The Lord told Moses to stretch out his hand to heaven. As Moses did so, a thick darkness blanketed the land. It lasted for three days. The Egyptians worshipped the sun in the sky as a god named Ra. It was one of their most important gods. But now, the one, true God, who had created light, made everything dark, showing them who was truly worthy of worship.

This frightened the pharaoh again. He brought Moses to him and asked him to leave but told him he must leave all of his flocks behind—for the plagues had killed the Egyptians' flocks but spared the Hebrews'. Moses refused, and Pharaoh's heart hardened once again. This time he told Moses to leave and never see his face again.

So Moses left, agreeing with Pharaoh at last. "As you say! I will never see your face again!"

Based on Exodus 7:14–10:29.

Pharaoh finally **frees** the Israelites

Nine plagues, nine chances.
The Lord had spoken through Moses and acted against the stubbornness of the pharaoh. He had sent gnats, flies, boils, locusts, frogs, death, and hail, and he had turned water to blood. Through all of these, God had shown his authority not only over the pharaoh but over the most powerful forces of nature worshipped and honored by the Egyptians, including the sun itself.

Still, the pharaoh was stubborn, with a hardened heart. So now God would send one more plague, one final warning and devastation: the death of all the firstborn, from animals to humans.

The angel of death would be sent to take the firstborn of each household. So to spare the children of Israel, Moses and Aaron were to warn them, prepare them, and then tell them to ready themselves to leave Egypt. For this final plague would, God said, move Pharaoh once and for all. After this, he would beg them to leave his country. Knowing Pharaoh and knowing how he changed his mind, though, there would be no time to waste. It was possible that he would let them go and then change his mind again.

And so Moses and Aaron told the children of Israel to get ready.

First, they were to protect their own firstborn from death. Each household was to find a male lamb a year old without any blemish—clean and healthy. They were to get this lamb on the tenth day of the month, keep it until the fourteenth day of the same month, and then slaughter it.

The blood of the lamb was to be painted on the doorpost and lintel of each house, and the meat was to be roasted and then eaten with bitter herbs and unleavened bread—that is, bread without any yeast in it, so it cooked quickly, without needing time to rise.

It was not to be just any meal, eaten in the ordinary way, either. The family was to eat this special meal while standing up, wearing their traveling clothes and shoes and holding the staffs they would use to walk.

Why? Because on that night, the night of the special meal, God would be executing his judgment over all of Egypt and showing his power over their false gods, the gods they carved with their own hands, who could never do anything to protect them. The firstborn of every home would die—except in those homes marked with the blood of the lamb. Those houses would be passed over by the angel bringing death to the land.

The children of Israel got ready. They gathered the lambs. They mixed the unleavened bread. They packed their belongings, listened to Moses' words, and worshipped the Lord they trusted to overcome the powers that enslaved them.

Midnight came. At that moment, all the firstborn in the land of Egypt, from the firstborn of Pharaoh to the firstborn of prisoners and the firstborn of cattle—all were struck down. In the darkness of that night, Pharaoh, grieving, heard the cries of all the people of Egypt mourning as well, and he called Moses and Aaron to his palace.

"Go," he finally said. "Leave. All of you sons of Israel, go and serve your Lord as you said you wanted to—and take all of your flocks with you as well."

Hundreds and thousands of children of Israel gathered up their possessions. They strapped the bowls with the unleavened dough to their backs, they led out their goats, sheep, and cattle, and they began. They began their journey back home to the land God had promised them.

It had been four hundred years since the sons of Jacob, called Israel, had come to Egypt. They had arrived in this land because God had brought good out of human evil. Joseph's brothers had sought to harm him, but God had worked through that hurt to save many people through Joseph's gifts. The children of Israel had flourished, then been oppressed. Their freedom to live in peace and to worship the Lord had been taken from them.

Now, through another man's leadership, another man who had strengths and weaknesses, whose life had taken strange turns, God was leading them back home, to the land he had promised them long ago.

And as God told the people through Moses, just as they were never to forget the promises he made to Abraham, they must never forget this moment of freedom, of exodus, either. Every year, they were to share this meal again. During this month, on these days, they were to celebrate with unleavened bread, bitter herbs, and roasted lamb. They were to sing praise, tell the story, and share the food that had been prepared by the oppressed people about to journey to freedom. Every year, the children of Israel were to remember God's great love, protection, and faithfulness with this special meal, the Passover meal.

Based on Exodus 11:1–13:22.

Moses parts the Red Sea

Out of Egypt,
the sons and daughters of Israel rushed into the wilderness.

That night, death passed over their blood-smeared doorways. They gathered up their children and their flocks, and Moses carefully carried the bones of Joseph. Into the night they fled, trusting in God's promise.

Back in Egypt, cries rose from humble huts and great palaces as God's power over life and death was made clear to the proud.

Through the night, the children of Israel traveled. God led them in a pillar of fire, and by day he led them in a pillar of cloud. So they journeyed without stopping, racing away from Egypt toward the Red Sea.

For just as God said, the pharaoh had begged Moses and Aaron to leave, but then, just as God said, he changed his mind.

The pharaoh said, "What have I done?" He regretted releasing his slaves, the hard workers building his kingdom.

So he prepared his chariot and hundreds of others, and with his army he set out in pursuit of the children of Israel.

At last Moses and the children of Israel reached the mighty sea, the Red Sea. And the Lord told them to camp nearby and wait. Now they could see the great army of Egyptians behind them, pursuing them. They could see clouds of dust and feel the thunderous echoes of man and beast on the ground. Without their own weapons or chariots, they were afraid. Not for the first time and not for the last, they turned to Moses in fear and poured out their complaints.

"Why?" they cried. "Why did you take us away from the land of Egypt? It would be better for us to serve the Egyptians than to die out here in the wilderness!"

Through Moses, the Lord reassured the people. The God of freedom and promise reminded them of who he was, of his trustworthiness. He, not Pharaoh, was in charge. Through his mighty deeds, God would show his power to all, Israel and Egypt both.

So they waited. And the pillar of cloud that had gone in front of them drew around behind them, so the Egyptians couldn't see where they were.

Then, in the night, Moses stretched out his hand over the waters. All night, God drove a great wind over the sea and divided the waters, pushing the sea to either side and making a path of dry land. And the children of Israel crossed on the dry seabed, the water held back on their right and left. And they reached the other side in safety.

The Egyptian army was behind them, chasing them, determined to recapture the children of Israel and return them to slavery in Egypt.

But while the children of Israel had been able to cross on the seabed as on dry land, the chariots and horses of the Egyptians were heavy and got stuck. Their wheels were clogged with mud.

The chariot drivers tried to turn back, for they could see that the God of Israel was fighting against them. But it was too late for the Egyptian army, stuck there in the muddy seabed of the Red Sea.

Now God told Moses to stretch out his hand over the water once more. And those same walls of water—which God had held back for the safety of his people—collapsed. In the morning, the water rushed back over the chariots, the horsemen, and the charioteers.

All were lost. All were defeated by God's great power.

God had brought his people life and freedom through water—as he did at Creation when the Spirit breathed across the waters, as he did when he rescued Noah and his family from the Flood, as he did when the baby Moses was rescued from the waters of the Nile, and as he would do again for us through the waters of Baptism, offering freedom from sin, freedom from death. Offering life.

Now, for the children of Israel—one step closer to freedom, the great threat of Egypt behind them—it was time for a celebration. It was time to sing and dance in praise of God's mighty power and love. So Miriam, Moses and Aaron's sister, sang a hymn of triumph. She and the other women took up their tambourines, dancing and singing:

"Sing to the LORD, for he has
triumphed gloriously;
The horse and his rider he
has thrown into the sea"
(Exodus 15:1).

Based on Exodus 13:17–15:21.

God sustains Israelites **with** **manna** in the desert

In the desert, the people panicked.
Yes, the Red Sea had swallowed the pharaoh's chariots and charioteers, and the children of Israel were no longer being chased. But they were suddenly on their own. People who were used to slavery were suddenly free. They were God's people, but they had forgotten his ways.

It had been hundreds of years since God had made a covenant with Abraham. As God had promised, his descendants were many, like the stars in the sky or the grains of sand on the beach. But for generations, these children of Israel had dwelled far away from the Promised Land. They had been surrounded by pagan gods and ideas.

Their journey home to dwell in the fullness of God's promise would take many steps and last many years. It would take a long time because the children of Israel had a lot of growing to do. It wasn't their fault, but they were distant from the Lord's ways. It would take time—and even suffering—to bring them closer to God, to help them understand his covenant. Their journey wasn't only to Canaan. Their journey was, above all, to a place of trust and confidence in God.

That challenge began right away, after the waters of the Red Sea had swallowed up the Pharaoh's army. There in the wilderness, in rocky, dry places where crops didn't grow and water was scarce, the people began to be hungry and scared. They began to wonder if they'd done the right thing in believing Moses and following him.

"We're hungry!" they cried. "At least in Egypt we had meat and bread to eat. Out here in the wilderness, we are all going to die of hunger!"

The Lord heard the people's cries and answered them. He showed them sources of good-tasting water. He also told Moses to tell the people that he would give them plenty to eat. In the evening they would have meat, and in the morning they would have bread, and in this way they would know that he was God, caring and ready to save.

And sure enough, in the evening quail—little fat birds almost like small chickens—appeared in the camp, enough for everyone to eat.

In the morning, God provided a different kind of food for the children of Israel. When they awoke, the ground was covered with something like flakes. It looked like big pieces of frost, and the people had no idea what it was.

Moses told them to gather it up, enough for their families. No more, no less—nothing was to be wasted, but no one was to be greedy and take too much, either. Every day, they gathered it from the ground, and on the sixth day of the week, they gathered twice as much so they could rest, as God had done, on the seventh day.

The people called this food "manna." They gathered it, boiled it, and baked it. It tasted to them like wafers made with honey.

In this way, God's people began to learn that they could trust God to care for them. They didn't live by bread alone but by trusting God's word. For as long as they were in the desert, the manna would remind them of his power to save and protect, for this was only the beginning of a long journey. There would be many times over the next forty years—

for that is how long the journey to Canaan would take—when the people would be unhappy or scared. There would be many times when they would be confused and wonder if they had indeed made the right decision to follow Moses and Aaron. There would even be times when they would actually forget God again and turn to idols, trusting in carvings rather than in the Lord.

But for those forty years, the manna would remind them of how deeply God cares for his children. And many generations later, as Jesus told stories to those gathered around him, he would remind them of the manna that God sent to his children in the desert. He would recall this bread from heaven and announce some amazing good news: that God was once again sending manna from heaven. This time, the manna was food for hungry souls. And those who ate of the new manna, the Bread of Life, would never be hungry again.

Based on Exodus 16.

God reveals the Ten Commandments

After three months in the wilderness, the people of Israel reached a place called Sinai. There was a great mountain there, and God called Moses to meet him on the mountain. He had given the children of Israel the great gift of freedom from slavery. Now it was time for them to understand why. Now God would reveal, through another covenant, what their freedom was for.

A covenant is a solemn promise between people. God had made a covenant with Noah, promising never to destroy the earth with a flood again. He had made a covenant with Abraham, promising that

Abraham would be the father of a great nation and the world would find salvation and blessing through that nation.

Moses would be the one to climb Mount Sinai and meet God, but this covenant wouldn't just be between God and one person. It would be between God and the entire people of Israel, now and in the future. It would be a promise of faithfulness.

The one, true, all-holy God was present in mystery and power on top of the mountain. While the people waited down below, Moses climbed the heights, surrounded by a thick cloud, thunder, lightning, and trumpet blasts. Smoke rose from the mountain, the sounds of trumpets grew louder, and the Lord spoke to Moses in the thunder. And it was here that God gave Moses the gift of the Law: the Ten Commandments.

God had created human beings good, in his own image. We're all created by God to live at one with his will. That's a part of each one of us.

But because of sin, we forget what that means. It becomes hard to see the truth or to make the right choices. Like Adam and Eve, we are tempted by pride, and we give in. Like the Egyptians, we are tempted to worship the work of our own hands or natural objects instead of the one, true God who created all. We try to create our own world instead of living at peace in the world God has made.

The Law that God gave Moses on the mountain, those Ten Commandments and all that flows from them, are gifts from the Lord to keep us close to him. When we break these rules, we're breaking the nature that God created in us, we're breaking the bonds of peace and harmony he built into the world. Maybe we shouldn't need them. Maybe we should just know what is right and wrong. Because of sin, though, we don't. Living by the Ten Commandments, we are living as God intended our first parents to live back in the Garden.

And that's the covenant God made with the people of Israel through Moses on the mountain. That is the Law he gave them, the way of life that would really form them into his people. Living by the Law, they'd be the source of blessing for the whole world that he promised through Abraham.

Coming down from the mountain, Moses told the people about all that God was giving them and asking of them. God had brought them out of slavery. God had shown his power. God had been faithful. It was their turn. Would they obey?

The people answered, "All the words which the Lord has spoken we will do." Their answer was yes!

So Moses rose and built an altar, with twelve pillars, one for each of the tribes of Israel—the families of the twelve sons of Jacob. They offered oxen for sacrifice, but before the oxen were burned as a sacrifice for the Lord, Moses took the blood from the slaughtered animals and poured it into bowls. He threw half of the blood on the altar of sacrifice.

He read the Lord's Law to the people, and once again they said in response, "All that the Lord has spoken we will do." And then Moses threw the other half of the blood on the people.

"Behold," he said, "the blood of the covenant which the Lord has made with you."

Obedience to the Lord meant life, joy, and peace. Turning away from him would bring sadness and death.

Then, in the wilderness at Sinai, Moses prepared to go up the mountain and remain in the Lord's holy presence for forty days and forty nights. God had led the people out of slavery, he had revealed his Law, he had made the covenant anew. Formed by his Law of justice and love, his people could be that source of blessing to the world. They agreed. The children of Israel said yes. The way to life and blessing was through living according to who we really are, who God created us to be, revealed to the children of Israel there on God's holy mountain.

Based on Exodus 24.

Israelites worship a golden calf

After sealing the covenant with God, Moses returned to the mountain. But he stayed a long time, and the children of Israel were getting restless. They had questions. They were confused and a little afraid.

Up there, far in the distance, Moses dwelt deep in the Lord's presence. The people below could see signs of God's power. They heard thunder. They saw lightning, smoke, and clouds. But still they wondered. Back in Egypt they had been surrounded by symbols and signs of pagan gods in temples and in homes. They wanted to feel at home again. They wanted to feel safe. So they forgot the Lord's promises and turned to Aaron, Moses' brother.

"Make us some gods," they demanded. "We don't know if Moses is ever coming back."

Aaron let the people have their way. He told them to bring him all the gold they had, their bracelets and earrings and other pieces. He melted all of that precious metal, and out of it he made an image: a calf.

The people praised that calf made of gold. "Here are the gods that brought us out of Egypt!" They prepared to worship with a feast and a celebration.

Up on the mountain, God told Moses what was happening down below. Angry, the Lord said that the people had already forgotten the way he had called them to. They'd already turned away from the covenant! They'd made an idol, a false god, and were eager to worship something that had no power. God was very angry. This would be the end of these stiff-necked people, he said. He would bring a new, great nation from Moses alone.

But Moses spoke honestly in his prayer, as he had done since he first met the Lord at the burning bush. He begged God to spare the people, reminding him of his promise. The Lord relented, and Moses came down from the mountain.

As he came down, he carried the tablets on which God himself had written his commandments …

I am the Lord your God, who brought you out of the house of bondage …

Now it was Moses' turn to be angry. He approached the camp, and what did he see? Glimmering and glistening, raised up high, was that golden calf, made by human hands, being honored and worshipped.

You shall have no other gods before me …

He heard singing and saw dancing around the golden calf.

You shall not make for yourself a graven image …

"All that the Lord has spoken we will do!" they had said.

How quickly had God's beloved people, rescued and cared for, turned away. Moses, burning with hot anger, threw the tablets on the ground and smashed them at the foot of the mountain. Then he burned the golden calf, ground the ashes to powder, and made the people drink the ashes.

Moses asked Aaron why he had allowed this to happen. Aaron explained, but even so, Moses could see that more help was needed. He needed stronger leaders to guide the people and help them stay strong.

He called out to the people: "Who is on the Lord's side? Let anyone on the Lord's side come to me."

Remember that Jacob had had twelve sons. The sons and daughters of each of the twelve were considered a tribe named for that son. Now, hundreds of years later, when Moses cried out to the people, it was Levi's descendants who stepped forward to stand by Moses' side. Because they were faithful, the Levites would serve the Lord in a special way from now on, as a tribe of priests.

Moses returned to the mountain and prayed for the people. The children of Israel, weak and afraid, had taken their eyes off the Lord and forgotten his promises. It had been hard to stay faithful. Moses asked the Lord to forgive them or punish Moses with them.

But the Lord punished only those who had turned away from him. He told Moses to lead the others now and journey again toward the Promised Land. And God sent them his angel to guide them.

Based on Exodus 32.

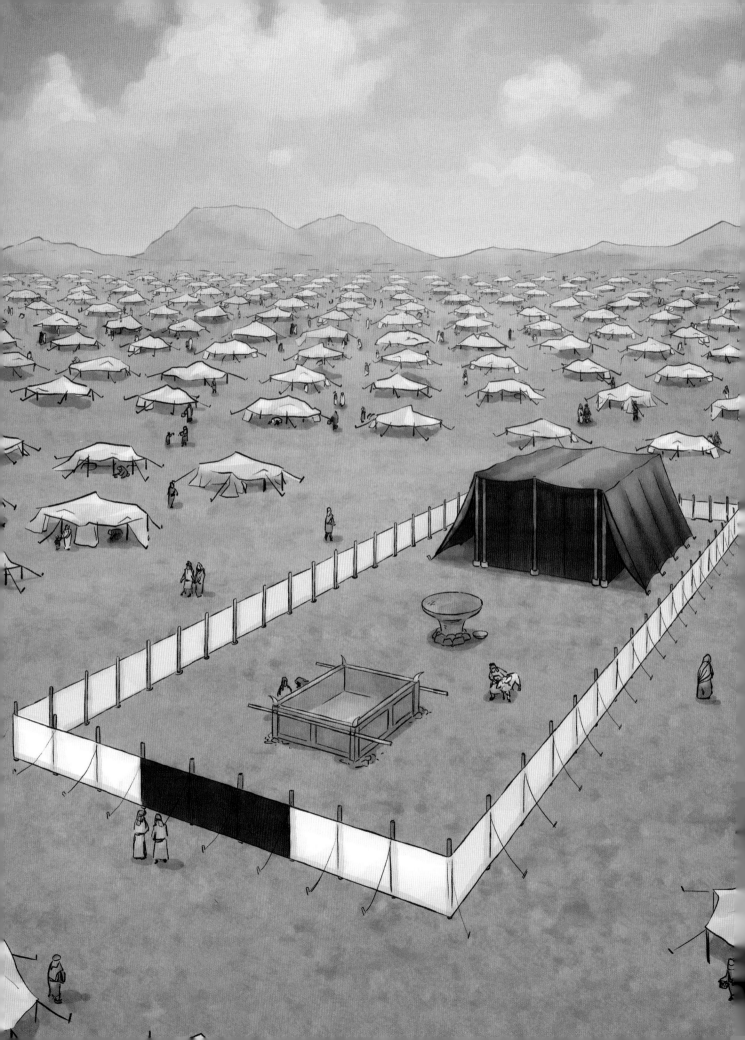

A tabernacle is built for the Ark of the Covenant

The children of Israel had stumbled badly.

Even so, the Lord wouldn't abandon them. He had made a covenant. The world cried out for blessing and salvation. These were the people chosen to share that blessing. Step by step on this journey, they would grow, they would learn, and they would be formed in God's image according to the Law he'd given them.

Moses returned to the mountain, where God wrote the commandments once again on tablets of stone. He passed near Moses and proclaimed his presence: "The Lord, the Lord, a God merciful and gracious, slow to anger and abounding in mercy and faithfulness."

Once again, not for the first time and not for the last time, God showered his mercy upon his children, his promise of love and forgiveness. And now he would give them a strong sign of his presence with them. They wouldn't feel alone again, as they had when Moses stayed so long atop Mount Sinai.

As they traveled to the Promised Land, they would carry the Lord's presence with them. It was time, Moses told the people, to build a tabernacle for the Lord.

The Tabernacle was a special tent, holy and sacred. Inside it was the Ark of the Covenant, which they would carry with them on their journey. The Ark would be a powerful sign of the Lord's presence on this long, hard trip.

When we honor the Lord and his mysterious presence among us, we just don't slap boards together and splash some paint. We love God above all things. What we give him reflects that love and his great glory, the best we can manage.

Moses called two workmen named Bezalel and Oholiab to design and craft the Tabernacle. The people themselves donated all the materials—the strong acacia wood, the lovely blue, purple, and scarlet fabrics, the precious stones, the oil and incense. Everyone helped, everyone had something to give to the Lord.

There were many parts to what the people were building for the Lord. There were the frames, made of strong wood and hung with beautiful fabrics. There was the tent that they'd set up for worship. There were the table and the altars, the lamps and the clothes for the priests and their helpers to wear when it was time to pray. And most important of all was the Ark of the Covenant.

The ark that Noah and his sons had built was a big structure that carried God's people to safety. This Ark was much smaller, but it also carried something precious: the tablets of the Ten Commandments and a container of manna. As the people carried this Ark through the wilderness, God would carry them to safety as well.

The Ark of the Covenant was beautiful and holy, covered in precious gold. Acacia wood poles were placed through gold rings on the corners when it was time to take the Ark on the journey. The lid of the Ark was the Lord's "mercy seat," made of pure gold. On either side of this mercy seat were golden statues of angels who faced it, their wings covering it.

God's people worked very hard and gave their best to the Tabernacle and the Ark of the Covenant. They used the most precious metal and jewels, the finest fabrics and the strongest wood. And when they had finished, they brought it all to Moses. And Moses blessed them.

When it was time to worship, Moses called on Aaron and his sons and anointed them as priests to serve the Lord in the Tabernacle. They washed themselves and put on their special garments. Lamps were lit, the sweet smell of incense rose to the heavens, and burnt offerings were made. God's people could see the tent hung with lovely fabrics. They could smell the incense and the offering.

But only Aaron, the high priest, could enter the innermost part of the tent, the Holy of Holies, the place of the Lord's presence above the Ark of the Covenant.

From that time on, the people could see that the Lord was with them as they moved through the wilderness. A cloud of the Lord's glory surrounded the tent, telling the people that the Lord was present. It was like the cloud that surrounded Mount Sinai when Moses met the Lord there. And it was like the cloud that would surround Jesus when he was transfigured—and again when he ascended to heaven.

God, loving and faithful, remained with the children of Israel. He remains with us. We still live on earth, though, seeing with only weak human eyes and reaching with weak human hands. We can, right now, only sense his presence through the mystery of an enveloping cloud as we journey to the place where we will someday see him face-to-face.

Based on Exodus 36–40.

DESERT WANDERINGS TIME PERIOD

1446 BC to 1406 BC

Israel's journey to the Promised Land takes much longer than anticipated. During the forty years God's people wander in the desert, they repeatedly rebel against God and Moses.

After **spies** scout Canaan, **trust** in God **wavers**

The children of Israel had remained for a year at Mount Sinai. They had built the beautiful Tabernacle and Ark of the Covenant for the Lord.

They finally moved on, traveling north. They were led by the Lord's presence going in front of them, letting them know when it was safe to go. God let them know that he was with them in the pillar of cloud during the day and the pillar of fire at night.

After some time, they were almost there! They were close to the land of Canaan, close to the land that God had given to Abraham all those centuries before, the land he had promised Abraham's descendants—these children of Israel, the women and men, boys and girls, who had traveled all the way from Egypt.

But what was Canaan like? Who lived there? The only way to find out was to send spies. So Moses called one man from each of the twelve tribes.

Moses told them to come back with a report. Were the people who lived in this land strong or weak? Were there a lot of them or just a few? Did they live in cities or smaller settlements? Was the land rich or poor? Was there wood on this land?

The men were gone for forty days, and what they had to say upon their return was a little frightening to hear. Yes, the land was rich and bountiful. It flowed with milk and honey. They brought back some of its fruit to share.

But the frightening news was that of course the land wasn't empty. People already lived there, and those people seemed very strong and powerful. There were Amalekites, Hittites, Jebusites, Amorites, and Canaanites. These people were strong, settled, and organized. It would be very hard to fight them.

Moses listened to the report along with the rest of the people. But confident in the Lord, he said they would move on into the land. Surely, they would be able to occupy it with God's help.

But most of the spies argued with Moses. Their words became more intense, and the picture they painted became more dangerous and dramatic. The land, they said, devoured its own inhabitants, and the people? They were so big and tall, the children of Israel would be like grasshoppers to them!

Hearing this, the people, not surprisingly, became very frightened. They cried out, they wept, and once again they complained to Moses and Aaron. Once again they said that it would have been better to stay in Egypt. Why had they come all this way and suffered so much only to be killed before they could even reach the Promised Land? It was time to go back, they said. Who would lead them?

Two of the spies disagreed with the other ten, though, and this was the moment to speak up. Joshua and Caleb stepped forward and tore their garments, a sign of grief and penance. They said to the people that, yes, the land was indeed rich and fertile and, most important, this was the land God had promised them. This was it. Did they believe his promise? God had said he would lead them here, and here they were. He said he would give them this land. Did they believe him?

Not yet, it seemed. For the people picked up stones from the ground and got ready to throw them at Joshua and Caleb.

In God's presence, Moses once again prayed for his people, the people God had sent him to lead. Yes, they were stubborn and disobedient. In spite of all that God had done for them, they still would not trust his promise. But that promise remained. Moses prayed knowing God would be faithful to it.

And he was. Faithful, full of compassion, he had forgiven them over and over, and he would again, right here.

But even when we are forgiven, even when our sins are in the past, we must still carry consequences, and so it was for the children of Israel. God had promised the people this land. He had promised that these people would be a source of blessing for the entire world. And they would be. God would do this.

But because of their lack of trust, because they had not remembered his faithfulness, they would be sent to wander again. For forty years, one year for every day the spies spent in Canaan, they would wander. No one over the age of twenty would ever set foot in the Promised Land. It would be a new generation to see it and settle it. And of the present leaders, only Joshua and Caleb, who called on the people to trust in the Lord's power, would enter the land they had glimpsed, that land of milk and honey.

Based on Numbers 13:1–14:38.

Aaron revealed as next leader

already, so many hard times. What a journey it had been so far!

The children of Israel had escaped from Egypt in the night, passing through the waters of the Red Sea, witnessing the mighty power of God. They had sung praise to God for what he had done but then turned away to worship a golden calf, the work of their own hands.

They had been afraid of going hungry and thirsty. God had provided for them. They had ached for signs of God's presence, and he had settled among them, guiding them through the wilderness by a cloud and by fire. They had complained and wondered why they'd left Egypt for these hard times, and over and over Moses had prayed and come to the people with the good news of God's mercy and help.

Trust him!

So they began their forty years in the wilderness, hundreds of people with their flocks and tents, trying to keep their hearts focused on God's promise. A hard thing to do for just one person, but imagine how difficult it is, in hard times, for so many to remember that they are one family, called to be faithful together.

People argued. People disagreed with Moses and Aaron. Aaron and Miriam disagreed with Moses. Some people wondered why they should obey Moses. They were angry and wanted to be the leaders themselves.

Moses, as he always did, went to the Lord. From the time God had come to him in the burning bush on Mount Horeb, Moses had never been afraid to be honest with God, to take every problem right to him, to ask questions about matters that were bothering him. Moses was always humble. He never forgot how small he was and how great God is. But he was also never afraid. He trusted God's promise, and he knew that the only way to get answers to hard questions and problems was to ask.

So what should Moses do now about those among his own people who were fighting him and wanting to take over instead?

God told him to tell the leaders of each tribe to get their rods and bring them to him.

Now, a rod was more than just a walking stick. For the people of this time, a rod was a symbol of authority. A shepherd used a rod to guide sheep safely to find water or food. With his rod Moses gave miraculous signs to the Egyptians. And it was Aaron's rod that turned into a snake in Pharaoh's palace and swallowed up the snakes of the court magicians. It was also Aaron's rod that had turned the Nile River to blood. With Aaron's rod, God had plagued stubborn Pharaoh with frogs and gnats.

So God said each of the tribes was to bring a rod, their sign of authority and leadership, to the Tent of Meeting, the Tabernacle. They were to bring them to the place where the Ark of the Covenant rested, where the children of Israel honored God's presence.

Then they were to write the name of their tribe on the rod, with Aaron's name written on the rod from the tribe of Levi. Lay those rods on the ground, the Lord said, and the rod belonging to the one whom I will choose to help lead will sprout green leaves. Then, God said to Moses, come to me in the Tent of Meeting.

So Moses did exactly what God asked, and each of the twelve tribes brought a rod to the Tent of Meeting. Moses laid them on the ground, close to the Lord's presence.

When he looked at them the next morning, indeed one had sprouted—Aaron's. Not only had it sprouted leaves, but it had produced ripe almonds as well. Through Aaron and his family, God would lead his people and bring good fruit and life to them.

When the people had suffered from hunger, God fed them with manna. As a reminder of God's power and care, they kept a container of manna in the Ark of the Covenant, along with the tablets of the Ten Commandments.

Now, they added a reminder of God's power to guide them. He had given them leaders. He had given them Moses to take them out of slavery, and he was giving them Aaron and his family to help Moses and lead them in worship and praise. Along with the tablets of the Law and the manna, they were to keep Aaron's rod, sprouting with the promise of life, to help them remember the one the Lord had chosen to help them on this long, hard journey.

Based on Numbers 17.

Moses strikes the rock; Israelites wander the desert

In the wilderness, the children of Israel thirsted. Their throats were parched. Their bodies ached for cool, clear water. Once again, they gathered and cried out to Moses and his brother Aaron. Once again, they remembered their lives back in Egypt, and as terrible as that had been, they complained that it must have been better than this!

"Why have you brought us here?" they demanded. "We can't grow anything in this place. We can't grow grain or fruit trees or grapevines. And the water! We have no water to drink! We'd be better off if we had died long before this!"

Moses and Aaron turned to the Lord, as they always did. They went into the Tent of Meeting and humbly fell on their faces in God's holy presence. Of course, God would provide for his people. God told them to gather everyone together in front of a large, special rock, and then tell the rock to bring forth water, and it would be enough for all to drink, enough for their thirsty livestock, too.

Moses and Aaron did as the Lord said. They gathered the people and stood before the rock. Moses lifted his rod, spoke to the people—and then he hit the rock with his rod. He hit it twice. Just as God had promised, water flowed from the rock. Everyone, even all the cattle, had plenty to drink.

But there was a problem. It wasn't a problem with the water, and this time, it wasn't a problem with the children of Israel. It was Moses.

For God had told Moses to bring water from the rock by speaking, as God had brought forth light and brought shape to creation through his word. He'd told Moses to speak and water would come out for the people and the livestock. But Moses did more than that. He struck the rock with his rod—twice. Because of this, God said, Moses would still lead the people to Canaan, but Moses would not enter the land himself.

Time passed. The journey continued. Along the way, the people of Israel met enemies and fought battles. They settled for short times and then began to move again. They were content, but then, time and time again, they complained. They wished over and over for the hard times to end, they wished they'd never left Egypt, and they questioned God's promise.

In the midst of this complaining, the children of Israel were reminded of how much it hurts us to trust ourselves instead of God. They were reminded of how painful it is to choose to turn away and stop listening to the Lord. Bitter, the people complained about the food and water they didn't have, and they even complained about one great gift they had been given: the manna God showered on them every day from heaven.

"We hate this worthless food," they said.

What pain the people felt now, as they rejected God's gift of life, especially sent for them faithfully each day. God sent fiery serpents among them. The serpents bit them and brought such great suffering that the people finally understood how ungrateful they'd been. They understood that they'd sinned against the Lord, and they begged for mercy. They asked Moses to please, please pray to the Lord and make the serpents and the pain go away.

So Moses did. He prayed, and God answered him. He told Moses to give the people a reminder and a sign. He was to make a serpent fashioned from bronze and set it up in the midst of the people. If anyone was bitten by a serpent, when they looked upon the image of the serpent raised above, they'd live.

They weren't worshipping the serpent—of course not! They weren't even trusting in the image made of metal to do anything for them. This wasn't magic. Only God can heal and save.

In calling the people to look at the image of the serpent lifted up before them, God was inviting them back to him, to listen and obey him. And centuries later, Jesus told a man named Nicodemus that just as Moses lifted up the serpent in the wilderness, when the Son of Man is lifted up, whoever believes in him will be saved.

Based on Numbers 20:1-13 and 21:4-9.

Joshua appointed to lead Israelites into Promised Land

The Lord, powerful and merciful, had brought his children out of Egypt and now, forty years later, they stood close to the Promised Land.

Along the way, they had been changed.

They had journeyed not just with their feet, walking rocky roads. They had journeyed with their hearts, too, listening and learning along the way.

For it was at the beginning of this journey that God had made his covenant with them. He'd given them his Law, the guidance they needed to be formed into the people he created them to be. If, as God told Abraham, they would be a source of blessing for the world, if they were the people through whom God would restore his creation, and if all the world would find salvation and life through Israel—they had to live it, didn't they? They couldn't go their own way and do what they wanted. They had to live as the Lord calls his creatures to live, in his image and likeness. The covenant and the Law taught them how to do this.

They'd heard that covenant proclaimed at Mount Sinai. They'd said yes to the Lord. Along the way, they had struggled with their faith and trust. They had argued and complained. They had sinned. But God remained faithful and merciful. And here they were. They had almost reached the Promised Land.

But not quite. In Moab, across the Dead Sea and the Jordan River from Canaan, on the same side of the river where Jacob had wrestled all night with an angel, the people came to a stop. Before they entered the land God had given them, Moses wanted them to stop and remember. It was time to hear the story again, of how and why God had brought them here.

So there in Moab, the Promised Land in sight, Moses gathered all the people. He told them the story again of how God had shown his power to Egypt and to them as well. He'd performed signs and wonders and overcome the great Egyptian powers and won their freedom. God had protected them in the wilderness and guarded them against those who would harm them.

Moses reminded them of God's covenant with them. His Law was the source of blessing. They carried it out in the way they lived and treated each other and in the way they worshipped God. Most of all, Moses said, because of these years in the desert—learning from the Lord, following him, and suffering—they carried the covenant and its promise in the deepest place of all: in their hearts.

Moses reminded them that God's word, the choice they had to make, wasn't far off. They didn't have to send anyone to the heavens or beyond the sea to discover it. The word of God, faithful, life-giving, and true, this life of love and communion with their Creator, was very near to them. It was in their own mouths and their own hearts.

And now Moses gave the people a choice. He told them God was asking them to choose. He had set before them life and death, blessing and curse. What would they choose?

"Choose life!" Moses called out to the children of Israel. "Choose life, that you and your descendants may live and dwell in the land God gave to Abraham, Isaac, and Jacob!"

Moses reminded the people of what God had told him many years before in Meribah. On that day, Moses had drawn water from the rock by striking it instead of simply speaking his word as God had said, and the Lord had told him he would never actually stand in the Promised Land. And so now, with his brother Aaron and his sister Miriam both dead, Moses needed to appoint a new leader who would guide the people to the land God had promised them.

And that would be Joshua! Joshua, son of Nun, who alone with Caleb had encouraged the people to trust the Lord even when they were frightened by the strength of those already living in Canaan. So Moses called Joshua to him and said, "Be strong and be of good courage! Don't be afraid, for the Lord goes before you and is with you."

Moses laid his hands on Joshua, and Joshua became their leader. And Moses blessed the people of Israel.

So Moses did not stand in the land God had promised his people. But he saw it with his own eyes. Once again, as he had done so many times before, Moses climbed a mountain in the company of the Lord. There in Moab, on Mount Nebo, the Lord showed Moses the land spread out beyond the city of Jericho and the Jordan River.

"This is the land," the Lord said, "that I swore to Abraham, Isaac, and Jacob for their descendants. Look, but you may not go."

And so Moses looked on the Promised Land, and there in Moab he died. And Joshua took up his leadership and readied himself and the people to move on, into the land so long promised by their faithful, loving God.

Based on Deuteronomy 29 and 31:1-23.

CONQUEST & JUDGES TIME PERIOD

1406 BC to 1050 BC

The Israelites finally enter the Promised Land under Joshua and conquer much of the territory, dividing the land among the twelve tribes of Israel. However, they still face their most important challenge of all: how to stay faithful to God.

Joshua parts the Jordan River

God spoke,
this time to Joshua.

"As I was with Moses," God assured him, "I will be with you."

Moses had died, and now it was time for Joshua to guide the children of Israel. Joshua was as close to the Lord as Moses had been, and he heard God tell him to be strong and have courage. God reminded him to stay close to him, to keep his mind and heart focused on the Law he had given, and to do all God commanded through the Law. If he did this, if he obeyed, he would have nothing at all to fear.

It was a new day with a new leader. A new generation had been born and was preparing to enter the land. But it was the same faithful God abiding by the same covenant and promise with them every step of the way. Joshua could remember how faithful God had been in the past, and he could look to the future without fear. He trusted God!

The Lord had given the people a great gift to help them remember all this: his presence in the Ark of the Covenant. Over many years they would struggle to conquer, settle, and rule the land God had promised Abraham and his children. And through that time Israel would find strength and courage in God's presence with them in the Ark. It began in this moment, as they prepared to cross the Jordan River.

All the people were gathered on the east banks of the river, with Canaan, the Promised Land, on the other side. Joshua told the people to get ready. They were going to see God do wonders, as he had done for their ancestors. They needed to prepare their hearts.

The Lord spoke to Joshua, as he had spoken to Moses so many times before. He told him what the priests should do next, and so Joshua, the priests, and the people obeyed the Lord.

The priests picked up the beautiful Ark of the Covenant, covered in gold, decorated with angels, carried on strong wooden poles. They began walking toward the river. God told Joshua that when the bare soles of the priests carrying the Ark were all under the waters of the Jordan River, something amazing would happen.

And so it did. Once again, as he had done at the Red Sea when the Egyptians pursued them, God caused the waters to stop flowing and make way for the children of Israel. Now it was the waters of the Jordan River that stood still, pulling back and rising up in a mighty heap in the distance. The riverbed was dry. God's people could cross on dry ground.

Once they were on the other side, the Lord gave Joshua more instructions. He told him to pick out one man from each of the twelve tribes of Israel and have them return to the river. Then each should pick up a stone from the Jordan and take it to the place on the other side where the people were camping. There, in that place called Gilgal, the stones would stand as a memorial, Joshua said. He told them that in the far future, when their children would ask why those twelve stones stood in that place, they could tell the story of how the waters had stopped before the Ark of the Covenant of the Lord. They could tell their children how God had dried up the waters of the Jordan River just as he had dried up the waters of the Red Sea in the time of Moses.

And so it was time to celebrate the Passover meal again, remembering all that God had done in the past and was doing now. And from this moment on, the gift of the manna was no more—it wasn't needed. The people would eat of the fruit of their own land now, the land of Canaan.

The story of God's power and goodness was not just for the children of Israel, though. Joshua reminded them that day that God had done this not just for them but for all the people of the earth. Through them, everyone would come to know God, their creator. Hearing the story, all the earth would know the power and the goodness of God. They would see it in God's care for the children of Israel. And from them, in time, the Savior of the whole world would come—Jesus, the Messiah, who would be baptized by John in the waters of this very same river.

Based on Joshua 3–4.

The Israelites see Jericho's walls crumble

God had promised
this land to the children of Abraham, who would one day outnumber the stars in the sky and the sand on the shore.

But the promise had been made a long time ago. Hundreds of years had passed, and now Joshua was leading the people to the land God had given them. But there were no welcome signs. Instead Joshua faced enemy settlements, armies, and walls.

The first great settlement they encountered was called Jericho. Like all large towns of that time, Jericho was surrounded by a tall, thick wall. In those days, people did not just come and go as they pleased. They did not travel from place to place and settle where they liked for the night. In a dangerous world, towns and cities protected themselves with walls and guards, careful of who they allowed inside.

Joshua had been sent as a spy many years before, and now he sent out spies. He selected two men and told them to enter Jericho and find out what they could about how strong the city was.

The two men traveled to Jericho and stayed at the house of a woman named Rahab. She was not, of course, one of the children of Israel, but she was kind to them. She knew that the spies were men of God. When she heard that the king of Jericho wanted to arrest them, she hid them on her roof.

Rahab told the men that the people of Jericho had already heard about Israel. They'd heard what God had done for Israel at the Red Sea. They'd heard about the battles Israel had won, and they were afraid.

Rahab told the spies to go into the hills for three days and hide from the people who were pursuing them. She also asked them to help her.

"Please," she said to them, "when you come back to our city, don't hurt my family. I've helped you. Will you please help us?"

The spies agreed and told her to tie a red cord in her window. When their army came into the city, the red cord would be the sign to leave her household alone.

After three days in the hills, the spies returned to Joshua and told him all they had learned. They assured him that the people of Jericho were weak and frightened, and the city would be theirs.

But even though the children of Israel were strong and the people of Jericho were frightened and weak, anything good they could achieve, like any of us, would not be by their own power. When we do good, it is because God gives us the gifts and the strength to do it.

Joshua was reminded of this when, near Jericho, he saw a man standing in front of him, his sword drawn. Joshua asked him if he was on their side or their enemies'. The man answered that he was the commander of the army of the Lord. Joshua asked what he should do, and the answer was simple: Joshua was to remove his shoes, as Moses was told to do at the burning bush, because where he was standing was holy ground.

When the time came to confront Jericho, the people of Israel didn't attack with

Joshua leads renewal of the covenant

Jericho had been taken.
Another city, called Ai, had been taken as well. The people of Israel, led by Joshua, were slowly crossing the land the Lord had given them in the covenant with their forefathers so long ago.

God had told Joshua from the beginning to keep the Law in his heart. He told Joshua never to forget that it was the Lord who had given all this to them and who sustained them. With God's help, they would stay strong.

To help the people remember God's goodness and mercy, to keep their eyes on the Lord, Joshua led them in worship. As Abraham, Isaac, and Jacob had done on their journeys, he made an altar. As Moses had done at Mount Sinai and on the banks of the Jordan River, he lifted up the covenant to the people and called on them to say yes to the Lord again.

Up high in a place called Mount Ebal, Joshua built his altar. It was an altar of rough, unhewn stones fashioned not by human hands but by God through nature. There the people offered burnt offerings to the Lord as they had done many times.

Joshua then took the stones, and on them wrote the Law that God had given his children. Everyone was there to see it—women, men, and children and even those who were not part of Israel but were traveling with them at the moment.

The people gathered at the foot of Mount Ebal, in the valley it made with Mount Gerizim. And in the midst of them was the presence of the Lord in the Ark of the Covenant.

All worshipped, all prayed, and all listened to the Law as Joshua read it out to them, the same Law that God had given to Moses years before.

At the center of the Law was the Ten Commandments, kept and treasured in the Ark of the Covenant. The Ten Commandments called God's people, young and old, to a life centered on honoring the Lord and respecting the lives and property of others, human beings made in God's image and likeness.

More laws flowed from this center. These laws were about every part of life. For God didn't just create some of us or parts of us. He doesn't only pay attention to us for a few minutes every day. He doesn't just love us once a week or care for us a few times a year. He created each of us, top to bottom, and every bit of us is made to reflect God's image and likeness—all day, every day, no matter where we are or who we are with.

As God had told Abraham, the covenant was with the people of Israel, but it wasn't just about them. It was about the whole world!

The world was to know blessing again through the children of Israel. The world, broken since the sin of our first parents in the Garden of Eden, was going to be knit back together. The world was darkened and twisted by the sin that killed Abel, that made the people of Babel so proud and brought the floodwaters pouring down from heaven. But the world would see light— through the children of Israel! So every bit of their own lives had to reflect what God wanted for his creation if the world was to understand and have the chance to say yes again.

So the Law was about every part of life. It was about the food they ate and how to cook it. It was about how to treat the poor. It was about how to help the sick. It was about how to live together in families and communities. It was about worship, sacrifice, and prayer. This is what Joshua read and the people heard again.

When God created the world, he said that everything he had made was good. Very good! The Law he gave Moses he gave so all the people of the world, everywhere and at all times, could see this goodness again.

Based on Joshua 8:30-35.

Israelite **tribes** **given** shares of **land in Canaan**

Long ago,

in the middle of a dark, frightening night, the people of Israel had fled Egypt. There they had suffered greatly, enslaved by one of the mightiest empires on earth. Now, many years later, they were in a much different place. Led by Joshua, they were conquering and claiming the land called Canaan.

They began from the east, on the far side of the Jordan River. Jericho and Ai were the first to fall, and then many other cities in the southern part of the land. All along the way, Joshua listened to God, who told him not to be afraid and helped him in many ways. God rained down hailstones on the enemy. At one point, God even made the sun stand still in the sky so that a battle could continue until the enemy was defeated.

From the east they moved south, then to the north. A few of the peoples they encountered made peace with them,

but many did not, so they fought battles along the way.

By the time Joshua reached old age, most of the land had been conquered. But not Philistia, on the coast of the Mediterranean Sea, or the area around the city that would be known later as Jerusalem. It would be King David, years later, who would take Jerusalem.

Now, with so much of the Promised Land won, it was time to divide it among the people.

God had promised Abraham that his descendants would be as numerous as the stars. The fulfillment of the promise had taken time, of course, and it had started from a very small beginning: with Isaac, then his two sons, Jacob and Esau, and then finally with Jacob's twelve sons.

By the time of Moses and then Joshua, the people of Israel were organized by which son of Jacob was their ancestor. So when it came time to divide the land among the people, that is how it was done: each of the twelve tribes got a part of the land to settle.

Moses had promised the tribes of Reuben, Gad, and half of the tribe of Manasseh land east of the Jordan River, where the campaign to win the land began.

Judah, Ephraim, and the other half of Manasseh were given land west of the Jordan River.

The other tribes all received their share: Simeon, Zebulun, Issachar, Asher, Naphtali, Dan, and Benjamin (Israel's youngest son).

And where was the tribe of Joseph, the son who saved all the others from hunger? Well, just before Jacob died, he blessed Joseph's two sons, Ephraim and Manasseh. This gave Joseph a double portion of Jacob's spiritual inheritance. That is why there is no tribe of Joseph, but there are tribes of Ephraim and Manasseh.

One more tribe remained: the tribe of Levi. The people of this tribe didn't get any land at all. This wasn't because they were less or were being punished. It's because they were special.

The sons of Levi, which included Moses and Aaron, were the priests of the people. They were the religious leaders who offered sacrifice on the altars, who led the people in worship of the Lord, and who protected the Tent of Meeting and the Ark of the Covenant. But now the people of Israel needed to worship wherever they settled. The Levites, the priests of Israel, couldn't be in just one place. So the Levites were given cities to live in, forty-eight in all, in the territories of all the other tribes.

After each of the tribes had received their portion and the land had been claimed, it was time, once again, to remember how and why they had reached this place. It was time to remember what all of this had been for: to dwell in this land and be formed as God's people, by his covenant.

So Joshua gathered the people at a place called Shechem. He reminded them of all God had done for them from the time of Abraham to the present day. He retold the story of God's protection and care for them and recalled the strength he gave them in battle.

Would they remember the Lord always?

Would they serve the Lord always?

Joshua asked the people this question. Who would they serve? Would they serve the old gods they had left behind and the many gods worshipped by the peoples surrounding them now, or would they choose the God who had created them, protected them, and brought them to this place?

"As for me and my house," Joshua said clearly, "we will serve the Lord!"

The people added their voices to Joshua's. They answered him, "Far be it from us that we should forsake the Lord!" They declared that they would be faithful, that they wouldn't serve other gods. Over and over, they said yes that day at Shechem, in a place where Joshua set up a great stone under an oak tree to remember.

"The Lord our God we will serve, and his voice we will obey!"

Based on Joshua 9–11 and 13–21.

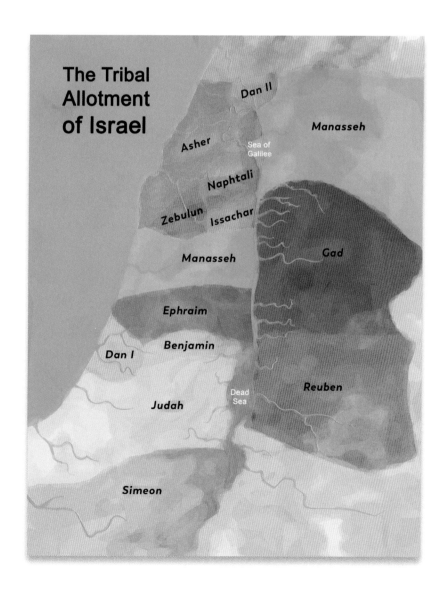

The Tribal Allotment of Israel

Samuel **anoints Saul** first **king** of Israel

For the people of Israel,
many old challenges had passed. They
were no longer enslaved or wandering.
They no longer had to wonder if they
would ever see the end of their journey.

Even though they faced new challenges
in Canaan, one old challenge had not
gone away and never would. It was the
most important challenge of all: how
to stay faithful to God.

In those early years, over and over, the
people went back and forth between
remembering and forgetting. Grateful to
God for a time, they would be faithful to

him. Then, afraid or tempted by the other
religions, they would begin worshipping
strange gods. Weak and distant from the
Lord who gives real strength and peace,
they'd suffer defeat and hardship—and
cry out to the Lord again for help.

And of course God never stopped helping.
In these early days of the new nation,
God helped by giving them leaders called
judges. These were men and women
God raised up to help the people of Israel
defend themselves and find peace again:
Gideon, Samson, and Deborah were three.

One of their leaders was the prophet Samuel. Before Samuel was born, his mother Hannah had prayed and promised that if she ever had a child, she would give the child in service to the Lord. So when her son Samuel was old enough, she gave him to Eli, the priest in charge of the Tabernacle at Shiloh.

One night, the boy Samuel was sleeping when he heard his name being called. He went to Eli and said, "Here I am!" But Eli hadn't called him, so Samuel went back to sleep. Again he heard his name. Again he went to the priest and was told to go back to sleep. The third time Samuel heard his name, Eli understood that he must be hearing the Lord. Eli told him to go back to bed but when he heard his name again to respond, "Speak, Lord, your servant hears."

And so Samuel did as Eli had told him, and the Lord spoke to him—just a boy. The Lord told him that Eli's sons had sinned, and because of them Israel was going to suffer. And that's what happened. For soon after, the Philistines attacked and defeated Israel and took away what was most precious to them: the Ark of the Covenant.

Later, the Ark was returned to Israel, and then Samuel, a grown man, called the people back to faithfulness in the Lord, their source of strength. Putting away their false gods, the people defeated the Philistines, and Samuel guided them as their leader for many years.

But like Eli's sons, Samuel's sons strayed from the Lord. They became greedy and took bribes. The elders of the people finally came to Samuel with a request. They didn't want to be ruled by judges and prophets anymore. They wanted something else. They wanted a king.

Samuel went to God in prayer. What should he do?

God answered that in asking for a king, the people weren't rejecting Samuel as their leader—they were rejecting the Lord. For a king is something more than a judge or prophet. Samuel and the judges made decisions and gave help that everyone knew really came from God. But a king? A king rules. A king is served by the people he rules. Ever since God called the children of Israel to be his own, they had served him alone, bound by the covenant and the Law he had given them. The Lord was their king.

But if a king is what they think they want, the Lord told Samuel, go and tell them what having a king really means.

Samuel told the people: "Here's what a king will do. A king will take your sons and make them serve in his army and support his household. A king will take your daughters and make them work for him. A king will take the best of your fields, crops, and flocks for his own. That's what you'll get with a king."

The people didn't care. They answered that all the other nations had kings—and if they were to be a great nation, they must have a king, too.

Samuel took this back to the Lord, who told him to give the people what they were asking for. Let them have their king.

So Samuel set forth to find the first king of Israel.

He had traveled to a town in an area called Zuph, when the Lord told him that the next day, he would be sending a man from the tribe of Benjamin—and that was to be Israel's king who would help them defeat the Philistines.

As the Lord said, the next day, a young man, tall and strong, came to the town—looking for his father's donkeys! He'd been up and down the land, searching for the animals, when he'd heard that the prophet Samuel was in this place. Perhaps Samuel could help him find the donkeys?

The Lord made clear that this young man, named Saul, was to be the new king. Samuel took Saul outside the city and told him. Saul argued that he was from the smallest tribe—Benjamin—but Samuel was sure of the Lord's will. So there, in private, he anointed Saul the first king of Israel.

Sometime later, Samuel gathered all the people together and told them that their new leader would be coming from the tribe of Benjamin and that the one the Lord had chosen was Saul. But when the people looked for Saul, they could not find him at first, for he was hiding among the carts and bags all the travelers had brought!

Samuel wrote down the duties of a king and the duties of the people, and Saul became their king.

Based on 1 Samuel 8:1-2 and 1 Samuel 9–10.

ROYAL KINGDOM TIME PERIOD

1050 BC to 930 BC

Although Israel becomes a united kingdom under Saul, the first king of Israel, Saul is not totally devoted to God. A great warrior named David becomes the second king and brings the Ark of the Covenant to Jerusalem. When David dies, his son Solomon takes the throne and builds a splendid temple in Jerusalem.

David defeats
Goliath the giant

Saul was now king of Israel.
But Saul's spirit was disturbed, restless and sad. Over the years, he stumbled as king. He disobeyed the Lord. He went his own way.

In time, the Lord went to Samuel and told him that even though Saul was still living, it was time to prepare for a new leader for the people of Israel. Samuel would find that new leader around the town of Bethlehem.

So as God directed, Samuel went to Bethlehem and to the household of a man named Jesse, who had many sons. It was from these young men and boys that God would call the new king of Israel.

When Samuel arrived in Bethlehem, he called all the people together, including Jesse and his family. He looked at all of Jesse's sons and saw one, tall and strong, and thought to himself that this surely must be the man God wanted him to anoint as king. But the Lord spoke to him: "Don't look at the outside," God said. "That's what people do. I look at the heart."

Samuel saw still more sons of Jesse—seven in all. None of them was the one chosen by God. Samuel asked Jesse, "Are all your sons here?"

Jesse answered that there was one more. The youngest son was out in the fields, tending the sheep.

"Send for him," Samuel said.

And when the young man appeared—healthy and handsome—the Lord made his will clear to Samuel. "Arise. Anoint him. For this is he."

The boy's name was David. Samuel anointed him that day with holy oil as the one the Lord had chosen to be the next king.

Sometime later, King Saul was nearby with his household and servants. By this time, Saul was often troubled by sad feelings and darkness. The only thing that could help him feel better was music. One of his servants had heard that David, son of Jesse, was skilled with the lyre, a kind of harp, so Saul sent for David. Coming into the king's presence, David played his music and sang, and for a time King Saul felt at peace.

Almost from the beginning of their presence in the land of Canaan, the people of Israel had come up against one great enemy again and again. This was the Philistines, a people settled on the seacoast. The people of Israel had battled them during the time of the judge named Samson, and it was the Philistines who had taken the Ark of the Covenant when Samuel was first in the service of Eli in Shiloh. Now the Philistines were on the move again.

They were camped on a great mountain in Judah, the southern part of the land. One of their most important soldiers was a huge man—a giant, almost—named Goliath.

Goliath was taller than anyone else on the battlefield. He wore strong armor from his head to his toes. He carried a great spear and was protected by a strong shield carried by another soldier. Goliath himself came out of the Philistine camp to challenge the army of Israel.

"Come out and fight!" he shouted. "Send one man to fight me! And if he can beat me, we will all be your servants!"

At this time, three of Jesse's sons were serving in Saul's army. But not David. He was still too young. He still spent his days tending sheep and running errands for his father. But on this day, his father Jesse had a job for him. He gave him some bread and cheese and told him to take it to his brothers in the field and share with their commanders as well. Then David was to bring back some sign from them so that Jesse, their father, would know that they were safe.

David traveled to the place of battle and found his brothers. At that moment, Goliath came out again with his battle cry, mocking the people of Israel and challenging them to find a man who would fight him. David saw how Goliath frightened the men fighting for Israel. He asked why they were frightened and what could be done about it. His question was repeated to Saul himself. Saul sent for David, and there David took his stand.

He would fight Goliath!

No one thought this was a good idea— not Saul and not David's brothers. Saul dressed him in armor, but the boy was too small for it and couldn't move. So David took off the armor and left the sword, but he held on to his slingshot and picked up five smooth stones for it. Then he moved out onto the battlefield to confront the huge, armed soldier.

When he saw the boy, Goliath was insulted.

"Am I a dog," he cried, "that you come at me with sticks?"

He continued to mock David, predicting that he'd soon be feeding his flesh to the birds and the animals.

David stood tall. David spoke bravely and directly. He told Goliath and all gathered where his strength came from: the Lord of Hosts, the God of Israel. On this day, David continued, it would be Goliath who would be fed to the birds and the beasts. And not for David's sake. Not so that everyone would see how great he was. No, this wasn't about David. It was about revealing the power of God: "The battle is the Lord's!" David said.

And so Goliath drew near. Quickly, David ran toward him. He put his hand in the bag on his shoulder and from it pulled a stone, which he placed in his slingshot. He slung the stone at Goliath and struck him in a place that was unprotected by all his mighty armor: on his forehead.

Goliath fell to the ground, dead. Great in worldly power, he had been brought down just as David said he would. He was defeated by the mighty power of God, acting through the surprising, sure hand of a shepherd from Bethlehem.

Based on 1 Samuel 16 and 17:1-31.

King David brings the **Ark** of the Covenant to **Jerusalem**

The city stood high on a hill.

The city had different names. Some called it Zion. Some knew it as the city of the Jebusites. We know it as Jerusalem. Now, at last, thanks to King David, it belonged to the people of Israel.

By this time, Samuel had died, and so had Saul. King Saul, anointed by Samuel as the first king of Israel, had had a sad and troubled life. He led Israel in battle, and as David grew older, David joined his brothers serving in King Saul's forces. David was a skilled fighter, and he helped the people of Israel defend themselves against all sorts of enemies. Because of this, David came to be loved, praised, and honored—even while Saul was still king. This made Saul jealous of David—so jealous that, at times, he chased David around the land, trying to take his life. But even when he had the chance, David didn't take any revenge on Saul.

Finally, King Saul died in battle, and David, long the Lord's anointed by

Samuel, took his place. Bit by bit, all the tribes of Israel, spread throughout the land, accepted David as their king, from north to south. And now at last, Jerusalem, the city on the hill, was theirs as well.

David understood, though, that the city did not really belong to them, mere human beings and creatures. It belonged to the Lord, the one who was their real ruler and king. Since God had spoken to Moses on Mount Sinai, the Lord had accompanied his people in a special way. For the children of Israel knew the Lord was present with them. They remembered the kind of life he called them to every time they saw the Ark of the Covenant in their midst.

They had carried the Ark of the Covenant through the wilderness on their journey to the Promised Land, and they understood God's presence there among them as they saw the pillar of cloud during the day and the fire at night.

So of course they would make a special place for the Ark of the Covenant in this most important city of Jerusalem—and David would lead the way.

When Moses saw the Lord in the burning bush on Mount Horeb, he'd been told to take off his shoes, for he was standing on holy ground. An angel had told Joshua the same thing outside the walls of Jericho. In the Lord's presence, we are humble. We remember how small we are and how great he is. We don't try to draw attention to ourselves. We give him the glory.

This is what King David brought to the Lord in Jerusalem that day.

David, a great warrior and anointed king, acclaimed by all the tribes of Israel, brought the Ark of the Covenant to the city, climbing the hills on dusty roads. He led a great procession, rejoicing. On the way, the people would stop and offer sacrifice and then begin again, playing music and singing. David himself was at the head of the people. He was not wearing armor or gold or sitting in a fancy chair. He was not surrounded by servants. No, dressed simply and standing tall, David sang, dancing and shouting with joy.

They brought up the Ark into the city and set it in a tent. David, acting as a priest now as well as king, offered burnt sacrifices to the Lord. He blessed the people, and he gave them special bread, cakes, and meat.

It was a joyful, happy day, but not everyone was pleased with what they saw. Michal, Saul's daughter and now David's wife, looked out and saw her husband leaping and dancing, and she was embarrassed and even a little angry. She told him that he had behaved foolishly, dressed more like a servant than a king.

David reminded her that God had chosen him to be king. She might be angry with him, but the servants she looked down on would surely praise the Lord with him—as indeed people everywhere have done ever since, praying the many psalms that came from his heart and his mouth, praising the Lord in song:

> "O sing to the LORD a new song;
> sing to the LORD, all the earth!
> Sing to the LORD, bless his name;
> tell of his salvation from day to day"
> (Psalm 96:1-2).

Based on 2 Samuel 5–6.

God makes a covenant with King David

David had always been close to the Lord.

When he was a boy, when he was a young man, and when he was a soldier in Saul's army, David always took his problems and questions to God. Before he made a decision, he asked God for guidance.

Now, as the king of all of Israel, David turned to God again.

Just as Samuel had helped Saul, so David had someone at his side to help him understand God's will. This man's name was Nathan. He was a prophet.

One day, David talked to Nathan about something that didn't make sense to him. David lived in a palace of cedar, strong and beautiful. But the Ark of the Covenant—the presence of God—was kept in just a tent!

The Ark itself, of course, was covered inside and out in gold, as God had directed in the time of Moses. But the Ark was kept in the Tabernacle, which was a tent, as it always had been.

This seemed right when the people of Israel were always on the move in the wilderness. But wasn't it time to build something solid and beautiful—a temple—to house the Ark of the Covenant? Nathan agreed.

That night, the Lord came to Nathan with a message for David, which Nathan shared the next day with the king. Through Nathan, God reminded David that the Lord had been with his people in a tent since their time in Egypt. He had traveled through the wilderness with them. Never once had he asked them to build him a temple. And after that, when they had stopped wandering, he hadn't asked their judges to build him a temple, and he wasn't asking David to do so now.

Instead, God said, he would establish David's house. The Lord was planting his people, and this is where they would grow. David had been a man of war, and it wasn't right for him to build God's house. Someday, in this place— here in Jerusalem after David died— David's son would build God's temple, and God would establish a kingdom ruled by David's offspring forever: the throne, the house, of David.

David heard this from the prophet Nathan. And David, humbled and grateful, prayed to the Lord. He praised God over and over for his goodness and protection, and he asked nothing more of the Lord than blessing for him and his house now and forever.

In this moment, the Lord made a covenant with David. He made a promise that David's family would grow, flourish, and be a source of blessing. Yes, a strong and beautiful temple for the Lord would be built someday, but a living home for God's presence was growing, too—within David's very own family.

It wasn't the first covenant God had made, of course. The Lord had entered into covenants with his people through Noah, Abraham, and Moses. Many times, the people had heard the covenant proclaimed and said yes to the Lord. They held this promise close in their hearts, as God had called them to: God would protect them and be with them. They would be his people. It would be through them that blessing would return to the broken world. The world would see God's mercy through his people's suffering, faithfulness, and love.

And so, as God promised, from the root of Jesse, David's father, the house of David grew. The men and women, fathers and mothers who branched out from that root worshipped and praised God. They did their best to follow him. Then a thousand years from the time of God's promise to David, not far from Jerusalem, the house of David would sprout a special branch.

God told David that one of his sons would establish a kingdom that would last forever. And so, in the tiny town of Bethlehem, where David, the shepherd king, had been born, angels would one day come to other shepherds tending their flocks in a field. The angels would have good news to share, about a special baby born of one of David's descendants, a son of the house of David whose kingdom would endure forever.

Based on 2 Samuel 7.

Solomon builds a splendid **temple** in Jerusalem

David lived to an old age and died in the city of Jerusalem, the city on the hill that he had conquered for God's people. Before he died, he spoke to Solomon, the son who would be following him on the throne.

He reminded Solomon to be faithful to God, to keep the Lord's commandments in practice and to keep them in his heart. And at the beginning of his reign, King Solomon did.

One night, the Lord appeared to Solomon in a dream. "Ask me for anything you like, and I will give it to you."

Solomon could have asked for wealth and power, but he didn't. He praised God for all he had done for his people, for his father, David, and for him. In this, the very beginning of his reign, King Solomon stood ready to guide the many people spread across the land, but he couldn't do it on his own. He needed wisdom. He needed the wisdom that only God can give.

So that is what he asked the Lord for: the wisdom to lead and always choose the good.

This pleased the Lord. Solomon hadn't asked for wealth or a long life for himself or even for the destruction of his enemies. He'd asked for wisdom— which is not just being smart and knowing a lot, but understanding with the mind of God, who made all things and knows what's best for us. So God, indeed, granted the new king that wise, understanding heart.

God had told David that it would be his son who would finally build a temple for him, and that is what happened. King Solomon, leading a nation mostly at peace and prosperous, began to guide the construction of a magnificent temple for the Lord in Zion, the city of Jerusalem.

What a change it had been from years past, when the children of Israel had fled for their lives from Egypt, carrying not much more than the clothes on their backs. Now, led by the Lord to this place, they dwelled in the land he had promised their fathers. Of course they wanted to honor him with the best they had!

King Solomon began with wood. In that part of the world, the best and strongest wood, cedar and cypress, grew in the land of Lebanon, north of Israel. Solomon sent to Lebanon for great timbers of cedar and cypress to make the walls and ceiling of the Temple.

The most important part of the Temple would be like the most important part of the Tabernacle: the place where the Ark of the Covenant would be kept. That place, the innermost part of the Temple, was called the Holy of Holies, and of course it would glimmer with gold.

The walls were overlaid with gold. Chains of gold marked its boundaries. The altar was lined with gold. Gold, precious and glowing, would remind everyone who saw it of God's glory, shining from the heavens, living in all of his creation, alive in the Law, kept safe there in the Ark of the Covenant.

Solomon saw that the Temple was decorated with images that would remind people of God's holiness. Great carved cherubim stood in the Holy of Holies, their two pairs of wings outstretched so that one pair touched the walls and the others touched each other, like arches over the sacred room. Walls were carved with cherubim and palm trees. The bronze pillars were adorned with carvings of fruit and lilies, reminding people of the Garden of Eden.

In a courtyard was an enormous bronze bowl called the molten sea. It had a brim like a lily, and it stood on the backs of twelve huge brazen oxen. Inside it were more than ten thousand gallons of water for the use of the priests.

It took seven years to build the Temple, seven years to make this beautiful place high on the hill, poised between heaven and earth. When it was finished, the people brought the Ark of the Covenant to the Temple in a great procession. And when the priests had placed the Ark inside, the cloud of the Lord's glory filled the Temple.

Solomon, son of David and the third king of Israel, the one who had guided the construction of the Temple from beginning to end, stood to make a speech and offer prayers.

As all of Israel's leaders had done when they spoke to the people, Solomon began by praising God and remembering all God had done for them. He praised the Lord for his mercy and his protection and for fulfilling all his promises to his father, David, and all the children of Israel.

This was the place, Solomon said, where they would now all come to seek the Lord's help. God wasn't far away. He was right here among them. In need, they could come and cry to the Lord. When they sinned and begged for mercy and forgiveness, God was here. When they suffered from drought or famine, the Lord was here to hear them. Even a foreigner could come to the Lord in his dwelling and offer his prayers.

Solomon offered sacrifices, and the people celebrated a great feast—but only after one more prayer. It was a prayer of gratitude and blessing and trust. In this prayer, Solomon remembered the covenant that God had sworn with their fathers, and the reason God had brought them to this place and poured out his blessing on them: so that they could be a blessing to the world—"that all the peoples of the earth may know that the Lord is God; there is no other!"

Based on 1 Kings 3:9-13 and 5:1–8:66.

DIVIDED KINGDOM TIME PERIOD

930 BC to 722 BC

After King Rehoboam treats his people
badly, ten tribes led by Jeroboam revolt
and become the Northern Kingdom.
Many kings of this period are unjust
and not faithful to God, but great
prophets like Elijah continue to call
the people back to God.

Jeroboam leads revolt; **kingdom splits** in two

God had made promises
to Solomon and the people of Israel—
and they, like their ancestors, had
made promises to God.

The Lord had promised that he would
be their God and they would be his own
people. And for their part, the children of
Israel promised, over and over through
the centuries as they heard the covenant
and the Law proclaimed, that they would
be faithful. They would live by the Law
that God had given them: they would

worship God alone, and they would
treat others justly. They would be a
light of goodness in the world.

The story of God's people is a long
journey of staying faithful, straying,
and returning to the Lord. In the desert,
the children of Israel listened, said yes
to the Lord—and then worshipped a
golden calf or complained about the
very manna God gave them to eat.

Later, as the people reached Canaan under Joshua's leadership, they again said yes to the Lord but then were tempted by the gods of other nations, tempted to forget the Lord who had done so much for them.

Even the leaders themselves strayed from God. The sons of Eli and then Samuel grew greedy. The first king, Saul, trusted his own wisdom more than God's guidance. The second king, David, committed a terrible sin when he took another man's wife for himself.

And now Solomon, David's son, was king.

King Solomon had asked God for wisdom. He had built the beautiful Temple for the Lord. But in time, Solomon too gave in to temptation and strayed. He grew rich and used his riches to build up a huge collection of horses—an important symbol of wealth at that time. He married many, many women. Many of these women were foreign, and they brought the worship of their false, foreign gods into Israel.

King Solomon also put heavy taxes on the people. This made some unhappy, and after Solomon died, the people came to his son Rehoboam, the new king. They begged him to lift their taxes.

Rehoboam told them to go away for three days while he considered their request.

King Rehoboam did think about it. He asked the older men who had been Solomon's advisors what to do. They told him to see himself as a servant to the people and speak to them with kindness. But his own, younger friends had different advice. They scoffed and told Rehoboam to go back and tell the people he was more powerful than his father had been. He should tell them that for their trouble, they'd now have even heavier taxes.

And that's what Rehoboam did. He told the people, "My father chastised you with whips, but I will chastise you with scorpions."

This cruelty of this new king was the beginning of the end of a united land. The vision and hope for all twelve tribes—the descendants of Jacob's sons worshipping the Lord together and flourishing in the land that God had given them—was shattered for the moment.

Meanwhile, Jeroboam, a leader from the tribe of Ephraim, had been in Egypt and was now returning. The people who were unhappy with

Rehoboam's rule turned to Jeroboam and asked him to lead them. They rebelled against Rehoboam, and the kingdom was split in two.

Jeroboam led the Northern Kingdom, and ten tribes followed him. This Northern Kingdom was known as Israel.

Only two tribes remained loyal to Rehoboam—the tribes of Judah and Benjamin, which were in the south, where Jerusalem was. This Southern Kingdom was called Judah.

Over the next few centuries, God's people, living now in the two kingdoms of Israel and Judah, continued to go their separate ways. They grew weaker and weaker as, once again, they strayed further from the Lord. At one point Jeroboam even made two calves of gold for the people to honor so they wouldn't be tempted to travel to Jerusalem.

There were some good kings, many bad ones, and great struggles. But along the way, God never stopped reaching out to his people. They had the Law in their hearts, if they would listen to it. They had the presence of the Lord in the Temple in Jerusalem, if they would just turn to him. And as they would see time and time again, they had prophets—men sent by God to warn, comfort, and guide them—if they would just open their hearts and listen.

Based on 1 Kings 12:1-24.

Elijah defeats the **prophets** of Baal

The kingdom had split in two, but God still called his people in both Israel and Judah, north and south, to be faithful to him. It would never be too late to return to him!

Throughout this time, God sent prophets to bring his people back. We have met prophets before. Samuel, who anointed the first kings, was a prophet. Nathan was the prophet who helped King David. And now, even with the kingdom divided, God sent even more prophets. Elijah was a prophet raised up by God to preach his word to one of the kings of Israel, the Northern Kingdom.

Elijah lived during the reign of the unfaithful king Ahab and his wife Jezebel. Elijah stood strongly and bravely against the king's worship of Baal, the false god his wife worshipped.

Elijah also warned the king that drought was coming to Israel, and indeed it did. The rains stopped for years. During this time, Elijah lived by a small stream where water still flowed, where day and night, ravens brought him food.

After a time, the drought was so bad that even the brook dried up, and Elijah went to find food. He ended up at the home of a widow, whom he asked for food and drink. She agreed, although, as she told him, she barely had enough to feed herself and her son. Elijah promised her that God would take care of them—and that's what happened. She used the last of her flour and oil to make Elijah a small cake, and miraculously her supplies of oil and flour continued for many days.

But that wasn't the only miracle. The widow's son grew ill and died. She was very sad and blamed his death on Elijah. The prophet took the boy's body to the roof, prayed to God, and God answered the prayer and brought the boy back to life.

After three years of drought, Elijah and King Ahab met again. Ahab called Elijah a "troubler of Israel." But Elijah turned the king's words around and said no, the king was the real troubler of Israel because he was leading the people away from God. The moment had come: the moment for Elijah to perform a mighty sign. The people needed the one, true God, not the false, empty gods that Ahab and Jezebel had brought to them. Elijah wanted the people to turn back to God, who could truly help and save.

What a challenge this would be. Jezebel had killed all of the Lord's prophets, and hundreds of prophets of the false gods stood against Elijah. He called them all to Mount Carmel, where two great bulls would be supplied for sacrifice.

On that day, the prophets and the people of Israel gathered. The prophets of Baal chose one of the bulls, killed it, and cut it in pieces for sacrifice. All day, they prayed to their god around their altar to send fire to burn up the bull, but nothing happened. They cried out and chanted their prayers. Still there was silence. Elijah mocked them. Perhaps Baal had fallen asleep? Or gone on a trip!

Elijah's turn came. He called the people to him and gathered twelve stones—like the twelve tribes of Israel. He made an altar from the stones, made a trench around the altar, and placed the pieces of his bull on it.

He told the people to bring water. They fetched the water in great jars, which

Elijah instructed them to pour all over the bull on the altar, and even over the wood that they had gathered to burn the sacrifice. And so they did. And then Elijah told them to do it a second time, and then a third! Everything—bull, stone altar, and wood—was soaking wet. Water pooled in the trenches around the altar.

It was time for Elijah to pray.

He praised the Lord, the one true God of Abraham, Isaac, and Israel. He told God that he was his faithful servant, that he had listened and done what the Lord had commanded. He begged God to answer his prayer—not to show off, not to demonstrate power so he could claim victory for himself, but so that the people would turn their hearts back to him, the Lord.

And God answered the prayer!

Fire fell from the heavens and everything burned: the bull, the stones, the drenched wood, and even the water in the trench. In gratitude and awe, remembering God's power to save, the people turned back to the Lord, and not long after that the drought ended, and the rain fell.

The king and queen were not happy, though. Jezebel threatened Elijah's life, and so Elijah journeyed into the wilderness. There, on Mount Horeb, he met the Lord in a different way. God had told him to stand on the heights and wait for him. A great wind rushed by and broke up the rocks around Elijah, but God wasn't in the wind. An earthquake came, and then fire, but God wasn't in either of those. Finally Elijah heard a still, small voice, and in that moment he knew it was the Lord.

Through Elijah, God worked in ways both great and small, in love and mercy, calling his people home.

Based on 1 Kings 16:30-32 and 1 Kings 18–21.

EXILE
TIME PERIOD

722 BC to 538 BC

The Northern Kingdom falls to Assyria in the year 722. A century and a half later, Babylon defeats the Southern Kingdom and destroys the Temple. During the upheaval and the exile that follows, the prophets remind the Israelites that God will not abandon them.

Northern Kingdom falls to Assyria

Hosea and Amos were two prophets who spoke God's word in Israel, the Northern Kingdom. They told the people of God's great love. They called them to be faithful to God and turn away from false gods. They told them that when they worshipped other gods, it was like a person in a marriage turning away from their husband or wife. They also reminded the people, over and over, that God didn't want them to be greedy. He was calling them to be generous and share with the poor.

Hosea and Amos and other prophets preached that God hadn't given the gift of the Promised Land so his people could worship other gods and keep his blessings to themselves. If they didn't change, they'd suffer. But the prophets also assured the people that the minute they turned back, God, like that loving spouse, would welcome them back.

The rest was up to them.

Would they say yes or no to the good things God was sharing with them? Would they pick from the forbidden tree over and over again like their first parents? Would they keep trying to live as if they didn't need God at all?

In that time and place, just like today, life was confusing and hard. The temptation to forget God and depend on human power alone was strong.

There in the Promised Land, the people were surrounded on all sides by great nations and empires. To the south was Egypt. To the north were the Assyrians and Syrians. These powerful nations were all on the move. They all, north and south, looked at the small piece of land God had given the people of Israel as a prize. To conquer this land would give the big nations control of the roads people traveled on from north to south and back again.

During the time of the first three kings—Saul, David, and Solomon—Israel was strong and united. It was able to hold its own against the other nations.

But under Rehoboam, Solomon's son, the nation had split into two. Israel became the Northern Kingdom, and Judah was the Southern Kingdom. Smaller and smaller, both of these kingdoms had to face great empires.

Would they listen to the prophets? Would they trust in God to protect them, or would they give in to human promises instead?

About the year 722 BC, Hoshea was the king of Israel, the Northern Kingdom. Shalmaneser, the king of Assyria to the north, threatened to invade Israel. To protect the country, Hoshea agreed to pay a tribute, or tax, to Assyria. But then Hoshea decided that Egypt could help him more, and he gave that money to Egypt.

In revenge, Shalmaneser invaded Israel. He put Hoshea in prison. He took many of God's people away from their land to Assyria. This was a common part of conquering other lands in those days. A conquering nation would remove defeated people from their lands. The conquerors made especially sure to take the richest and most powerful leaders so they could have their land and other possessions. They could also make sure that the people most likely to lead a revolt were far away.

The king of Assyria didn't leave an empty place in the land, though. He brought many of his own people to live there, as well as people from other conquered nations. He also feared God enough to bring a priest of Israel to them to teach them, even though they continued many of their practices of worshipping idols.

At that time, the most important city of the Northern Kingdom was called Samaria, and the people who lived there came to be known as Samaritans. Even up to the time of Jesus, they lived and worshipped with a mixture of traditions that were not in line with the Law of Moses. That is why the Jewish people at the time of Jesus looked down on the Samaritans, because they considered the religion of the Samaritans impure. It is also why, when Jesus wanted people to see how great the love of God really is, he would use a Samaritan as an example.

But long before Jesus' time, Israel, the Northern Kingdom, was gone. The ten tribes who had been given the land in Joshua's time had been given a great gift. But instead of living there faithfully, they worshipped other gods, ignored the needs of the poor, and took on the customs of other nations. They trusted their own pride more than God, and now their kingdom was gone. The prophets had warned them. The prophets had spoken to them of God's love.

The rest had been up to them.

Based on 2 Kings 17.

Babylon defeats Judah and destroys the Temple

The Northern Kingdom of Israel had fallen, but in the south, tiny Judah still stood.

All around Judah and its capital of Jerusalem, kingdoms were battling. Assyria, which had brought down the Northern Kingdom, had itself been conquered by the great Babylonian empire.

But in Judah, at least for now, Solomon's temple still stood. The Ark of the Covenant rested in the Holy of Holies. Kings from the House of David still reigned.

Some of these kings were faithful to the Lord. Hezekiah and his grandson Josiah both removed foreign gods and all the unfaithful, harmful practices that came with them. But other kings, like Ahaz and Manasseh, actually encouraged the people to worship foreign gods. They even allowed the people to do terrible, harmful things.

But as he always does, the Lord remained faithful to his people. He kept sending prophets to warn, to comfort, and to help. The prophets—men like Isaiah,

Jeremiah, and Ezekiel—listened to the Lord.

Over and over, the prophets reminded the kings and the people that their strength was from the Lord alone. Trusting human beings and false gods instead might seem to make them stronger, but it didn't. If they continued to cut themselves off from the Lord, the source of their strength, they would become weak and would fall.

But even if they did, the prophets also reminded the people, God wouldn't abandon them. Even in these hard times, God's promise was sure. He had made a covenant that promised them life and hope, and he would keep it. Most important, these prophets said, the Lord's promise was about more than this time and this place. God's promise was about peace that would never be broken by war again. It was about a feast that would never end. Could the people keep their eyes on that future, no matter what happened here on earth?

The challenge to do this was great. For in time, more than a hundred years after the fall of the Northern Kingdom, the powerful Babylonian empire faced Judah.

The Babylonian king was Nebuchadnezzar. He gained so much power over Judah that he was able to force many of the richest and most skilled inhabitants to move away to Babylon. He did this to make his own nation stronger and to discourage rebellion in Judah.

One person did rebel though, and it was an important person: the king of Judah, Zedekiah. In answer to King Zedekiah's rebellion, King Nebuchadnezzar of Babylon sent his armies to attack Jerusalem. They surrounded the city, so no food could get inside. King Zedekiah did escape, though, but he was captured near Jericho and taken as a prisoner to Babylon.

With the ruler of Judah gone, it was time for Babylon to show the people left in Judah who was in charge. The Babylonians started with the destruction of Jerusalem. They put their sights on the most sacred, important place for the people of Judah: the Temple.

They broke the bronze pillars that supported the Temple. They took away all the gold and silver vessels. They killed the priests who served the Lord. There weren't many people left in the city by then, but whoever remained was captured and sent into exile in Babylon.

It was a tragic, confusing, and terrible time for God's people. Even though they had been warned time and time again, it was still hard for them to understand why this had happened. Hadn't God promised them this land? And now it was taken from them, and they were taken away from it, too. How would they worship without the Temple? How would they worship and live as God's children away from the land he had given

them? Their sadness was so deep, it is remembered in a psalm:

> "By the waters of Babylon,
> there we sat down and wept,
> when we remembered Zion …
> How shall we sing the Lord's
> song in a foreign land?
> If I forget you, O Jerusalem,
> let my right hand whither!"
> (Psalm 137:1, 4-5)

Based on 2 Kings 25.

Daniel interprets the king's dreams

The Northern Kingdom was gone. Over one hundred years later, the Babylonian empire brought down the Southern Kingdom, too. Led by their king Nebuchadnezzar, the Babylonians took land and cities from God's people. Finally, they took the people as well. They made them travel far away from their homes to live in exile, in distant Babylon.

One of those people was a young man named Daniel.

Daniel was part of the first group of exiles brought to Babylon from Judah.

Skillful and smart, Daniel and three of his friends—Shadrach, Meshach, and Abednego—were brought to live in the king's palace. There, they would be educated for three years and would serve the king.

As a part of that wealthy household, the young men were expected to eat the rich foods of the Babylonians. But through Moses, God had given the people of Israel the Law. A very important part of the Law was about what foods they were allowed to eat. Daniel and his friends wanted to be faithful to God and to the Law. They refused to eat anything but vegetables or drink anything but water.

This made the king's servants afraid. They thought for sure that if Daniel and his friends didn't eat the rich Babylonian food, they'd grow weak, and then the king would be angry at his servants for not taking good care of them. Daniel made them a promise. Daniel was sure that if he could obey God's Law and eat only the food that God allowed, he'd end up stronger, not weaker. Give him ten days, he said to the servants.

And indeed, at the end of those ten days, Daniel and his friends were as healthy and strong as ever, ready to keep learning and growing in the household of King Nebuchadnezzar.

Now, King Nebuchadnezzar was troubled by strange dreams. He brought all of his own magicians and sorcerers to him. He demanded that they help him understand these dreams. But he didn't tell them what his dreams were about. That was how the king would know if they really had a deep understanding of these mysteries: They would not only tell him what the dreams meant, they would tell him what they were!

The royal magicians and sorcerers tried to delay the king by asking for hints. But this angered the king so much that he decided to have the magicians and sorcerers killed. Daniel's life was in danger, too. He went to the head of the king's guards and pointed out another way: a way of mercy. He asked for a chance to interpret the king's dreams himself. But could he do it?

That night, Daniel had a vision. In the vision, the king's dream was revealed to him. When he woke up, Daniel sang a prayer of praise to the Lord. He praised God, who is all wise and shares that wisdom with those who love him. He praised the Lord who gives us strength and reveals the truth. Daniel was ready to go before the king.

First, Daniel told King Nebuchadnezzar about God. He told him that there was one Creator of heaven and earth. No human being could reveal mysteries like another person's dreams. This wisdom could only come from God.

Then Daniel related the king's dream: In it, he'd seen a huge figure. It had a head of gold, a chest and arms of silver, a belly and thighs of bronze, legs of iron, and feet partly of iron and partly of clay.

In the dream, a stone, not cut by a human hand, struck the image's feet and broke them. After this, the rest of the figure was struck so that all the pieces broke apart. They were all carried away like the lightest part of grain after threshing, never to be seen again. But the stone that destroyed the image? It grew into a great mountain that filled the entire earth.

He was right! Yes, that was the king's dream, and now Daniel would tell him and the whole court what the dream meant.

King Nebuchadnezzar was the head, made of gold. After his reign, another kingdom would arise. Represented by the silver, it was not as powerful. After that came a kingdom that was even less powerful, like the bronze. A kingdom strong like iron would rise next. This kingdom would crush many others, because that's what iron can do. Then a divided and mixed kingdom— like the feet of both iron and clay— would rise. But this kingdom would break because it, too, was weak, since iron and clay don't mix well.

We now know that one day, all of these kingdoms—the Babylonian, then Persian, then Greek, and then Roman empires—would be gone. Then God, who was the stone with the power to break them all, would reign. The kingdom of God would be brought to earth by Jesus during that last earthly empire that Daniel had seen. It would be stronger than any of the others, and it would last until the end of time.

Based on Daniel 2.

RETURN
TIME PERIOD

538 BC to 167 BC

After decades of exile, the Israelites are allowed to return to their homeland, where they rebuild the Temple in Jerusalem. Although it's difficult, key leaders and prophets guide the people to rebuild the city and their lives according to God's Law.

Israelites return to Judah and rebuild the Temple

God's people had been in exile for fifty years. It was at last time to go home to Judah.

Human powers come and go. Empires rise and fall. So Babylon, which had conquered Judah and sent the Jewish people into exile, was conquered itself by a new power: the Persian empire.

Cyrus was the king of Persia, and right away, he had surprising news for God's people. He was going to let them go home!

King Cyrus issued a decree. He was allowing the exiles to return to Judah from Babylon. Not only could they return, but they could take with them the precious gold and silver items that Babylon had stolen from the Temple. He would even give them help to start rebuilding the Temple!

It would take many years, but the journey home had begun.

The second temple would not be as glorious as what Solomon had built and the Babylonians had broken into dust. But even though they were poor and no longer a power among the other nations, God's people could still give the Lord their best.

Cyrus appointed a man named Zerubbabel to be governor of the first group of the Lord's people to go back to Judah. Zerubbabel was helped by Jeshua, the head priest. Once they arrived in Jerusalem, they immediately set up an altar and offered burnt offerings to thank God. They even celebrated a feast, the Feast of Booths, which Jewish people still celebrate today to give thanks for the harvest and to remember how God helped their ancestors in the wilderness.

It was time to get busy. Zerubbabel sent workers north to Lebanon, as Solomon had done, to get strong timbers of cedar and cypress wood. Other workers laid the stone foundations for the new temple. When they did, the Levites, or priests, came with trumpets and song, celebrating just as King David had when he brought the Ark of the Covenant to Jerusalem. The people sang, the people shouted—they were so grateful to be back and to be able to serve the Lord in freedom again. Their celebration was so loud that everyone in the city could hear.

But not everyone in the city was happy. Some people who had been living near Jerusalem came to offer help, but Zerubbabel sent them away, saying that this was their own work for the Lord and they would do it themselves. This angered the people who had offered help. They wrote letters to the king of Persia, now a man named Artaxerxes. The letter writers told the king that what the Jewish people were doing was surely the start of a rebellion.

While everyone waited for the king's decision, construction came to a stop. It saddened the people to have to leave the Temple unfinished, but as he always did, God sent comfort. Prophets like Haggai and Zechariah encouraged the people. They told them to have hope and trust:

"Rejoice greatly, O daughter of Zion! Shout aloud, O daughter of Jerusalem!" (Zechariah 9:9).

After years of problems, the people finally decided to simply start building again. Again the people living nearby tried to stop them by complaining to the king— now a new king named Darius. They said the king should search the royal records. Had King Cyrus really allowed this? But Zerubbabel and his helpers continued, confident that the decree from King Cyrus would eventually be found.

And it was! King Darius wrote back to those who had complained. He said yes, the Jewish people had permission to build their temple again. But that wasn't all. Darius told the governors and other leaders that they had to help now. They were to help pay for the cost of rebuilding. They were even to supply wheat, oils, salt, or wine the priests needed for worship of the Lord.

With all of this help, the people managed to finish the Temple. Passover was drawing near. Passover celebrated the time when God's power freed the Jews from slavery in Egypt. Now they had another reason to celebrate in the Promised Land, where God had led them once again.

The first journey of God's people, from Egypt to the Promised Land so many years ago, had been more than a trip from one place on earth to another. It was also a journey to greater understanding and closeness to God, as the people of Israel learned about the Law and grew in the Lord's covenant. This journey home after exile and this rebuilding was more than just a trip, too. It was more than just a welcome return to a once-familiar place. And now, more than homes and walls would have to be rebuilt. Hearts would have to grow in love, questions be answered, and hope restored. Like that first journey, this one would take a long time.

Based on Ezra 3–6.

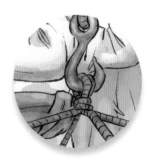

Ezra leads the **people** back to the Lord

Rebuilding the Temple

for the Lord in Jerusalem was important and good. Rebuilding hearts was important, too.

God's people had suffered very much. They had suffered because others had treated them cruelly. They had suffered because rulers wanted more power and land. But they had also suffered because they had turned away from God. Over the years, they had put faith in idols. They had become weak. They forgot God's promise, and their hearts grew sad. They lost hope.

The walls of the second temple would be strong and beautiful. How would the hearts of God's people become strong, too? Who would help them?

A man named Ezra answered the call.

Ezra was a Jewish scribe and teacher living in Babylon. He did not travel back to Judah right away when King Cyrus let people return. Even when the Temple was being rebuilt, he still lived in Babylon. There he studied God's Word and grew in wisdom.

But after a number of years, King Artaxerxes of Persia asked Ezra to return to Judah. He told Ezra that his job was to teach people about God's Law. He gave Ezra gifts of gold and silver for the Temple. He also gave Ezra the job of choosing leaders for the people. These leaders would rule by God's Law.

Many people returned with Ezra. They trusted in the Lord so much that they refused to ask the king for protection on their journey. Instead, they fasted and prayed. They put all their trust in God.

When they safely arrived, they saw that all was not well in Judah. Yes, they were able to share the king's gifts with the Temple. Yes, they could worship. They could offer sacrifice and prayers to the Lord. But as Ezra looked and listened to the way God's people were living, he could see that he had a lot of work to do.

God had given the Law to Moses on Mount Sinai. Every step of the way, God's people had listened to the Law and promised to obey. But they hadn't heard the Law read aloud in a long time. They'd forgotten it. They'd fallen away from the Lord.

The first problem Ezra saw was that many of God's people had married foreigners. This was a problem because the foreigners brought false gods and bad practices with them. First a family here or there would begin to worship false gods, and then whole communities would start.

Ezra spoke about this to the people. He told them how sad it made him to hear that they were honoring false gods. Because of this, he had prayed, fasted, and even torn his clothes. He had thanked God for bringing them home, but he was still afraid. He was afraid that because so many had turned from the gift of the Law, they would never be strong again. He wanted the Lord to be honored and worshipped with hearts that loved only for him. Ezra prayed and told the Lord how sorry he was that the people had turned away from him.

The people heard Ezra's prayer and were sorry, too. They listened, prayed, and wept. Their ancestors had heard Moses and Joshua proclaim the Law and had promised to obey. Here, back in Judah, God's people promised, too. They agreed to set aside all that kept them from God. Their hearts would belong only to him.

It was an important step. They had rebuilt the Temple. They had begun worshipping the Lord again. They were offering sacrifice and celebrating feasts.

But as the prophets had told them through the years, these things were good, but God was promising more to those who loved him. There was another Zion to look to. This Zion wasn't on earth. It wasn't a city built by people. It was built by the Lord alone. The Zion that God was leading them to was life with him forever. There the Law wouldn't be written on stone—it would be deep in their hearts.

Joshua had told God's people of this promise years before. The prophet Ezekiel had foretold it, too. Ezekiel had suffered during the Exile in Babylon, and God had shown him this Zion that would last forever. There, God would do something wonderful. He would raise flesh from dead bones. He would change and rebuild not just what was on the outside but what was inside, too:

> "A new heart I will give you, and
> a new spirit I will put within you;
> and I will take out of your flesh
> the heart of stone and give you
> a heart of flesh"
> (Ezekiel 36:26).

Based on Ezra 7:1–8:36, 9:1, and 10:1.

Queen Esther saves her people

God's ways are so often the opposite of human ways. He calls men and women who seem unimportant and asks them to do his work. He turns the wrong that people do into chances for the good to shine through. God can do anything, anywhere.

And so, in Persia during the Exile, God used a young woman named Esther to save his people, not just from slavery this time, but from death.

There was a king named Ahasuerus who reigned from a city called Susa, in what we now know as the country of Iran. He was seeking a wife.

Mordecai was one of the many Jewish people living in exile in that area at the time. His cousin was a beautiful young woman named Esther. Mordecai helped Esther become one of the young women who would be considered to be the new queen. And after many months, she was indeed chosen to sit on the throne by the king's side as his new queen.

One day, Mordecai was standing outside the gates of the palace when he overheard two men plotting to murder the king. Mordecai told Esther, and Esther warned the king. So the criminals were caught and punished, and Mordecai's help was made known to the king.

Haman was one of the king's helpers, a prideful man who expected honor because of his position in the palace. As he walked around the city, he assumed that everyone he passed would bow down to him, and most did—but not Mordecai. As one of God's people, Mordecai didn't give that kind of honor to anyone but the Lord.

This enraged Haman, and he decided to punish Mordecai and all his people— all the Jewish people living in exile. So Haman spoke to the king and described the lives of the Jewish people in the worst way. He made it sound like they sought to disobey the king when in fact they were trying to live by God's Law. He told the king that the kingdom would be stronger and better without them. The king believed him and wrote a decree calling for the deaths of all the Jewish people, women and men and even children.

Mordecai heard of this. He began to grieve and mourn. He tore his clothes and put on sackcloth and ashes—signs of great sadness—and many of the Jewish people followed him, doing the same.

Esther heard of the decree, she heard of her people's distress, and she, too, began to mourn. She sent messages to Mordecai. What should she do? He told her that she should simply ask the king to change his mind. Esther sent another message, reminding Mordecai that with this king, no one—not even the queen—could just walk up to him to ask a question or a favor. You had to be called by the king to speak to him, and she had not been called into his presence for a whole month. If she took it upon herself to enter his presence, she too might be killed, just for that.

But the threat to her people was very great. So Esther asked Mordecai and all her people to pray for her. "Hold a fast for me," she begged. "I'll fast, too. And then I'll go to the king. If I perish, I perish."

Both Esther and Mordecai prayed, begging God to give her courage and help, to use Esther to save her people.

Full of the courage that comes only from the Lord, Esther approached the king. She asked simply to have a dinner party.

Who would come? Esther, the king, and Haman. The king agreed, and it was time to prepare.

Haman was quite excited and pleased with himself. He went back to his home and told his family that great things were about to happen. He was going to dinner with the king and the queen! He had enjoyed great honors so far in the palace, and surely even better things were coming. There was still that matter of Mordecai, though. As long as Mordecai lived, Haman couldn't really be happy.

Well, his wife said, since you're seeing the king, take that moment to ask him to kill Mordecai. Haman agreed that this was an excellent idea, and he ordered gallows to be set up right away—gallows for hanging Mordecai.

The night before the dinner, the king couldn't sleep and was reading through some old records. He noticed what the man Mordecai had done for him and wondered if Mordecai had ever been honored for saving the king's life. At that moment Haman came in, and the king asked him, "What should be done for a man the king would like to honor?" Haman thought, "He's talking about me!"

So Haman described all the great things that should be done for a man like that: royal robes, a royal horse, and a royal procession for everyone to see. That, the king answered, is a great idea. And so he gave it all to Mordecai.

It was time for the now very surprised Haman to go to dinner with the king and the queen. There, the king asked Esther what her request was, and she told him everything. She told the king about the plan to kill the Jewish people—and she told him Haman was to blame. Enraged, the king ordered him to be hanged. And so Haman was hanged on the gallows he had built for Mordecai.

So the people's lives were saved, and they were allowed to live by their own law, the Law the Lord had given them on Mount Sinai. And it was all because of God's working, as he does, in a surprising way through a surprising person—a young woman named Esther.

Based on the book of Esther.

Nehemiah and Ezra rebuild Jerusalem

Nehemiah was a Jewish man who lived in exile in Babylon. He was a cupbearer for the king. One day King Artaxerxes noticed how sad Nehemiah looked. He asked him why.

Nehemiah told him all that he had heard about the problems God's people were having in Judah. They had been allowed to return and were glad they could begin to rebuild the Temple. But other people were living in Jerusalem now too, and some of them didn't like that. They had tried to stop the Temple from rising again. It saddened Nehemiah to hear all of this.

He told the king that he wanted to return to Judah. He wanted to help the people so they might be safe against those who were trying to drive them away. The king gave his permission, and Nehemiah set off.

When he arrived in Jerusalem, what he saw was mostly ruins. The walls of the city had all collapsed, and no gates remained standing. The city and all the people in it were unprotected. Anyone could come and go. Anyone could enter and do harm or damage.

So Nehemiah decided to get those walls raised high again.

It was a big job. Everyone from every family had to help. Nehemiah divided up the work and gave each family a section of the wall or a gate to repair. They piled up stones, high and strong. They made bolts and locks from metal for the gates. They created doors of strong wood.

But some people who lived in the area were still angry. They didn't like to see God's people building a strong wall to protect themselves. They tried to attack the workers. Nehemiah had a plan for that, too. He told the people that some should keep working but keep weapons to protect them nearby. Others should keep watch. Everyone should always be listening. Everyone should be ready to rush to help in case one section of the wall was attacked.

Finally, the wall was finished. It was time to thank God, worship and celebrate. It was time to praise the Lord, who had always been faithful and strong!

Ezra, the scribe who had been teaching the people about the Law, was still in Jerusalem. He called the people to the Water Gate in the city wall. Women and men, young and old gathered there. Ezra stood on a platform and shared the Law that God had given Moses with all the people. He read every word of guidance that God had given on Mount Sinai. The people heard the Law, and they remembered the ways that God called them to worship him, to eat, and to live together.

Ezra and Nehemiah worked together to rebuild the walls of Jerusalem and the hearts of God's people who lived there. The people worked with Nehemiah to rebuild their walls. And they listened to Ezra as he taught them about the Law again. They listened once again to the wonderful story of all God had done for his children, from the time of Abraham to Moses and to that very moment. They listened, they remembered, and they agreed. They would obey the Lord's commandments. They wouldn't marry foreigners. They would keep the Sabbath day holy. They would give the first and the best of their crops and animals to the Lord. They would give to the Lord through the Temple and its worship.

God's people prayed. They were sorry for the times they'd forgotten God's goodness, the times they'd turned away from him. They asked him to forgive them. Strong walls were protecting them once again. The Temple stood tall and beautiful on Zion. God's people were ready to say yes to the covenant again.

Based on Nehemiah 3:1–4:23 and 8:1-12.

MACCABEAN REVOLT TIME PERIOD

167 BC to AD 1

Antiochus tries to destroy the Israelites, but a small army of Israelites known as the Maccabees revolts and over time manages to drive the Greeks out of Jerusalem. Israel becomes an independent kingdom again for about a hundred years, until the Romans take over in 63 BC.

Antiochus
seeks to destroy
God's **people**

God's people had journeyed, learned, ruled, and suffered. Over the centuries, since first being called and formed by the covenant with Abraham, they had tried to follow the Lord in all kinds of circumstances.

They had freely answered God's invitation and found their way to settle in Canaan. They had been enslaved in Egypt. They had journeyed in the wilderness. They had fought battles. They had settled and ruled. They had been conquered and sent into exile.

The Jewish people had lived in all kinds of times and places, but through it all, God was faithful. They might live in different places under various rulers, but God never changed. His Law didn't change. His covenant with his people didn't change. God was always faithful, always ready to forgive and give his children promise and hope.

Now, hundreds of years after the return from exile, back in the land he had promised them, God's people were in great need of hope.

They had suffered before—in slavery, in confusion and hunger, and in exile. But this was different. For now, a power had come to their own land, determined to rip them away from God himself.

His name was Antiochus IV, and he had come to rule the land from the empire of the Greeks.

Alexander the Great was a powerful ruler who had, in his short life, extended the Greek empire to almost the whole boundaries of the known world—even to India! As often happens, after his death, people fought about who would be in charge next. Two sets of leaders ended up splitting the empire between them. One was based in Egypt, south of Israel, and the other was based in Syria, which is just to the north. Antiochus IV was the ruler who came to Judah from the north, ready to destroy.

He entered the beautiful city of Jerusalem. The first temple had been destroyed by the Babylonians. But when God's people returned, they rebuilt it and, led by Ezra and Nehemiah, rededicated themselves to the Lord. The second temple was smaller, but it too stood tall and beautiful, a place to worship the Lord and offer praise for all he had done, from giving life to saving his people.

None of this mattered to Antiochus. He saw just two things: riches and competition. Of course he wanted the wealth of the Temple for himself—the cups and bowls and candleholders and the gold-lined walls that glorified God. But he also wanted to take away, in any way he could, the ties that the Jewish people had with God and the way of life God had given them. It was a special way of life. It set them apart. Because of it, the Jewish people would not honor a worldly leader like Antiochus in the way he thought he deserved. Faithful to God, they were a sign to worldly rulers that, as powerful as they were, there was Someone even more powerful who ruled the universe.

Antiochus was determined to destroy it all.

So he began. He stripped the Temple of its precious vessels and decorations. After a time, he set about plundering the city itself, destroying people's homes and even the city walls that Nehemiah had planned and helped build. Antiochus brought in his own people and built his own walls and buildings.

The way of life God had given his people was not confined in buildings, though. They could follow him no matter where or how they lived, and so Antiochus next turned to this. He made laws requiring the Jewish people to eat foods that God had declared unclean in the Law of

Moses. He required them to sacrifice to pagan idols and to work on the Sabbath. The life that God had given them was to be left behind, or they would die.

Antiochus went even further. He took the books of the Law that were found throughout the land and had them destroyed, the scrolls torn and burned. Anyone caught with a holy Jewish book was killed. Pagan altars were built in the Jewish communities, and incense was offered to false, pagan gods in every neighborhood. There was nowhere to turn.

Not even, now, the Temple. In a great act of hatred and sacrilege, Antiochus had a statue of a pagan god erected in the Temple itself.

In fear and in hope of saving their own lives, some of God's people gave in. They made the sacrifices to pagan gods, they ate the forbidden food, and they tried to fit in, to live like Greeks, accepting the ways and cultures of those around them.

But not all. Many resisted, and many died.

A number of foods were forbidden by the Law given to Moses, but one of the most important was pig's flesh, pork. That, along with shellfish and the flesh of a few other animals, was not to be eaten ever.

So of course, under the Greek rule of Antiochus, the Jewish people were being forced to eat pork.

One family refused. A mother and her seven sons boldly announced that they would never eat pork. Enraged, the king maltreated the brothers one by one. But before they died, the brothers and their mother spoke out bravely. They said that, though their tormentors had power on earth, it was nothing compared to the power of God, who had created them out of nothing, who was faithful and would give them life again. Even the great emperor, with all his worldly power, stood helpless before the Lord of life. The mother and her sons, facing death, were full of hope, knowing that God is ready to save all who love him and are faithful to him. And so they died, all seven brothers and their mother, trusting God and eager for the life to come.

Based on 1 Maccabees 1:20-62 and 2 Maccabees 7.

Maccabees restore the Temple

Antiochus did his best
to destroy God's people. Everything they rebuilt after their Exile, he tried to take down. Every sign of the covenant, he had worked to wipe out. Some people bravely resisted, but others gave in, trying to save their lives by blending in with the world around them.

Would this be the end of the journey for God's people?

No, not with a man named Mattathias, his sons, and a small, brave army.

Mattathias had five sons. Grieved to see the destruction of Jerusalem and the Temple, mournful and outraged that Antiochus had set up pagan gods to worship in God's holy house, Mattathias planned a revolt. He and his sons fought the Greeks. And when Mattathias died, his son Judas Maccabeus took command. The odds were greatly against this little army, for their numbers were so small and they didn't have the wealth and strength of the Greeks. But they did have the Lord, and to him Judas Maccabeus prayed over and over, remembering moments in his people's journey when it had surely seemed that all was lost but God had helped them prevail.

And over time, the Maccabees were able to defeat their enemies and drive the Greeks out of Jerusalem.

They had won. Jerusalem was theirs again. What would be the first thing to do? Rebuild houses? Set up shops? Plant crops?

No. The first, most important thing to do was to honor God: to rebuild his temple and make it, once more, a beautiful place to worship the Lord who had given them life and hope.

Judas led the army up to Mount Zion where the Temple stood, and what they saw there was ruin. All the decorations were gone. The gate was burned. The altar of sacrifice had been used for pagan offerings.

Bushes and trees grew up among the rubble. All the rooms of the Temple were ruined, tumbled down and broken up.

Judas Maccabeus told his men to help, and he got to work. He called priests to come back to the Temple, and there they talked about what to do about the altar. Since Antiochus and the Greeks had offered sacrifices to false gods on this altar, would it ever be fitting to use it again for the Lord? No, it wouldn't.

So they set aside the stones of that altar and built a new one with stones uncut by human hands, just as Jewish leaders had always done.

Then they set about the hard work of rebuilding and redecorating the Temple. They made new vessels and brought in lamps. They burned incense, placed bread on the table of offering, and hung curtains to protect the holy places.

It was time, finally, to celebrate. Like David when he brought the Ark of the Covenant to Jerusalem eight hundred years before, like Ezra and Nehemiah leading the people in celebration upon the return five hundred years after that, God's people came to the hill called Zion to praise, worship, and honor the Lord. They offered sacrifice on the new altar. God's people returned, processing, singing, and playing music on all their instruments: harps, lutes, and cymbals.

For eight days, they celebrated. For eight days they offered sacrifices in the Temple. And Judas Maccabeus declared that this, like Passover, was special enough to remember every year. And so, even today, the Jewish people celebrate the feast called Hanukkah, eight days of prayer, feasting, and candles, to remember God's faithfulness always.

* * *

It had begun with a word. It had begun with God's word, spoken into the nothingness: *Let there be light.* And then, amid all the other beauties and mysteries of his creation, God made a special creature, made in his own image and likeness, made to live in communion with that loving Creator.

Man and woman, created by their loving God, chose to turn away from him, though. Their children wandered the earth, learning, growing, settling, and creating. Their feet wandered, and so did their spirits, far from the life of love and harmony God had designed them for.

But God didn't turn from them. He held out a promise: his covenant. A covenant made with Abraham, Moses, David, and all his people. A covenant of love and strength: *I will be your God, and you will be my people.*

God's people said yes to the promise. They tried to live by it; they failed and rejected it.

God didn't turn from them.

Again and again, working through ordinary women and men of all kinds, working through shepherds and kings, mothers and fathers, soldiers and hermits, and even working through human weakness, sin, and failure, God reached out.

He reached out and he called, he beckoned and invited them to return to him. Sometimes he even pulled. Over the years, his people came to understand more deeply. They repented, changed, and grew in wisdom. They heard the words of prophets who told them that yes, the land God promised is important. And yes, it is important to worship the Lord with words—but another time is coming.

This new time, the prophets proclaimed to the people, is what God has been preparing you for the whole time. All the suffering, all the questions, even all the mistakes point right here. The journey you've been on has led you to the real glory of what God has been promising all along: hope, love, life, safety, and peace. He has promised that this time will never, ever end—there will come a temple that will never be destroyed, a city on a hill that will never fall, a feast and a celebration that will fill you forever, and a law that will be written deep in your hearts.

God never broke his promise, the prophets proclaimed, and he won't break it now. He is coming to us, walking as close as he did when Adam and Eve were still in the Garden. He is about to pitch his tent among us, bringing news. The best news. The Good News.

Based on 1 Maccabees 4:36-61.

MESSIANIC FULFILLMENT TIME PERIOD

AD 1 to AD 33

Jesus, the Son of God, becomes man and enters the story of Israel. He calls twelve apostles and gathers many disciples as he proclaims the Good News of the kingdom, teaches, and heals many. Jesus dies on the Cross to save mankind, rises from the dead, and ascends into heaven.

The angel **Gabriel** **visits** a virgin named **Mary**

Such a long family history we have!

Our first parents, created in God's image, were given all they needed to live in happiness and peace in the Garden of Eden. But Adam and Eve turned from God. They had to leave that place God had specially prepared for them.

But God didn't leave his children to wander. He called them and invited them back to his arms. Over and over, through Abraham and the prophets, from the land of Ur to Egypt and all over Canaan, he guided, welcomed, and forgave them. He made covenants and promises; he sent prophets. The Lord never forgot his people.

And now the people, God's people, lived very differently than they had before. Spread out over the known world, most of them lived under the rule of a new and powerful empire: the Roman Empire.

The rebuilt temple still stood in Jerusalem, and the people still practiced their faith. They tried to observe the Law that God had given Moses. They listened to God's Word and prayed in synagogues. And under the rule of a foreign hand, they waited.

God's people waited and remembered. They remembered all the beautiful prophecies God had given them through great men like Isaiah and Ezekiel: prophecies of a time when they would live in true freedom, never hungry or thirsty again, when the lion and the lamb would lie down together in peace, led by a little child.

It was for this child they waited. Messiah, they called him: one chosen and anointed by God, who would come to them, suffer with them, and save them. They didn't know when or where, and different people had different ideas about who a messiah would be and what he would be like. God's people wondered about that, and waited, in hope.

Now, in this moment of waiting and watching for a leader, under this powerful empire, there lived a very young woman who loved God. She lived in a humble dwelling in a village in the north of Israel called Nazareth. Her name was Mary.

One day, Mary was in her home when an angel came to her. The angel's name was Gabriel. He greeted Mary.

"Hail, full of grace! The Lord is with you."

You won't be surprised to hear that Mary was a little troubled by this greeting. An angel was with her, speaking to her in her house! Gabriel comforted Mary. He told her not to be afraid at all. He was there because she had found great favor with God. The angel had come with wonderful news: Mary was going to have a son, and his name would be Jesus!

More than that, her son would be very special. Gabriel told Mary that Jesus would be called the Son of the Most High. God would give him David's throne, and his kingdom would never end.

This puzzled Mary even more, and she wasn't afraid to ask Gabriel about it, starting from the beginning of the problem: She wasn't married. How would she have a child?

This wouldn't be a problem for the Lord. The Holy Spirit would overshadow Mary, and the child would be the Son of God.

The angel told her that God was working in another woman's life, too. Mary's cousin Elizabeth, who was much older, was also pregnant now. "For," the angel said, "with God nothing is impossible!"

Long ago, in the Garden, Eve had said no to God. And now God was reaching out to the world through Mary, a new Eve. What would she say?

"Let it be done to me according to your word."

Mary said yes. She said yes to God's invitation. She said yes to trust in him. She said yes to God's presence at the center of her life. There, in a small home in a small village far from big cities and great powers, this one young woman said yes. She said yes to the Messiah.

This was big news. And what do we do when big news happens in our life? We want to share it. So Mary went right away to the person who could best share in this news: Elizabeth, her cousin who, the angel said, was also expecting a baby.

After a long journey to the south, Mary arrived at Elizabeth's home in Judah, the region where Jerusalem was.

Elizabeth saw Mary coming, and as she rushed to greet her, Elizabeth felt something new. Deep inside her, the baby she had been carrying for six months now—leaped!

"Blessed are you among women!" Elizabeth cried out to Mary. "And blessed is the fruit of your womb!" She knew that Mary's baby was very special, because the baby inside her—Jesus' cousin John—recognized him.

What a moment of joy. Mary, like the Ark of the Covenant, was carrying the Lord within her, and the first person to recognize him was another baby in the womb, John. Filled with life and with joy, Mary sang. She sang a hymn of praise to the Lord that we still pray today. We call it the Magnificat, which is the Latin for the first word of Mary's song of joy and gratitude for all God had done for her—and for all his people:

"My soul magnifies the Lord, and my spirit rejoices in God my Savior!"
(Luke 1:46-47)

Based on Luke 1:26-38.

A Savior is born

Mary and Joseph were on a journey.
They were going to Bethlehem!

Bethlehem is a very small town near Jerusalem. It is the place where King David was born, centuries ago, and it was because of David that Joseph and Mary were traveling there.

God's people, the Jewish people, didn't have their own nation anymore. They were spread out in many places, most of them under the control of Rome.

The Roman emperor was Caesar Augustus, and he wanted an exact count of the people in his empire. In this time, before telephones and computers, the only way to count people was to see them face-to-face. To do this in an organized way, all the people had to go to the city of their ancestors. For Joseph, who came from the line of David, that city was Bethlehem.

So Mary and Joseph made their way to Bethlehem with many, many others. It was a slow journey, because it was close to the time for Mary's baby to be born—the baby the angel Gabriel had announced.

But when Mary and Joseph arrived in Bethlehem, there was nowhere for them to stay! There was no room in any of the inns, so they settled down in the only spot they could find: a place like a stable, perhaps a cave, where animals like goats, sheep, and horses were sheltered.

Not all the animals were in the stable that night, though. Nearby, sheep grazed and slept in the fields, and their shepherds watched and protected them.

The night was dark and deep. And into that darkness, God (as he always does) sent light. The shepherds saw lights in the sky, they saw movement and heard singing, and they were puzzled and afraid. What was happening?

It was angels! And the angels were singing, bringing the news that all God's people had been waiting for. They brought it not to the emperor or the wealthy merchants but to poor shepherds keeping watch in the hills.

"Don't be afraid!" the angels said. "We're bringing you good news of great joy! Today, in the City of David, a savior has been born. He is Christ the Lord!"

The angels told the shepherds where they would find this child, wrapped in swaddling clothes and lying in a manger, a feeding trough for animals. And then, filled with joy, the angels sang, "Glory to God in the highest!"

And so the shepherds rushed to Bethlehem and found the baby lying in a manger. It was Jesus, the newborn king, with his mother, Mary, and his earthly father, Joseph.

Just as the angel Gabriel had said, Jesus was born of Mary by the Holy Spirit. Joseph had taken Mary as his wife. But in this great, deep, beautiful mystery, Joseph wasn't Jesus' father: That was God. God the Father.

Jesus, Christ the Lord, is the Son of God! He was certainly a very real baby, lying in the manger helpless and needing to be fed, just as you and I were when we were first born. But at the same time, he was fully God, from the moment the angel spoke to Mary in Nazareth to the moment he was born and to eternity.

So the angels sang, the shepherds came and saw, and Mary pondered everything deep in her heart.

The birth of this child was amazing and hard to believe, yes, but some people understood immediately what God had done.

Forty days after Jesus was born, Mary and Joseph took Jesus to Jerusalem, to present him to the Lord in the Temple. They brought a pair of turtledoves for sacrifice, and in the Temple they met two people who had been listening to God for a very long time. Like all God's people, these two had heard God's promises to send a savior. They had studied and listened; they had opened their hearts and watched for signs.

Simeon was one of them. He was an old man. The Holy Spirit had told him that he would not die before he saw the Lord's Messiah, the Savior. On the day Mary and Joseph brought their baby to the Temple, Simeon knew right away who Jesus was.

"Lord," Simeon prayed as he took the baby Jesus in his arms, "let your servant go in peace now, for my eyes have seen your salvation and the light for the world!"

The other person who understood was a very old woman named Anna. She was a prophet who stayed in the Temple all the time, fasting and praying. Her spirit was always listening for God. When she saw Jesus, she thanked God with joy, because she knew right away that this baby was the Messiah. And she told many others about him.

God had kept his promise. From the time Adam and Eve and their children and their children had turned away from him, when they chose to disobey and make their own rules, God had promised forgiveness and mercy—and had poured it out.

He had promised to be close to his people through his covenants—with Noah, with Abraham, and with Moses and David. He had shown his power in mighty deeds and had guided the people by the words of his prophets. He had traveled with them and protected them, making his presence known to them in the cloud and the fire and the Ark of the Covenant.

The Lord had come closer and closer, inviting them to let him transform their stony hearts into hearts that can love.

And now he was here as one of us. He was a baby now but would soon be a boy and then a man—a man who would walk and talk with us, listen to us, teach us, and laugh with us. He would set us free.

In the beginning, God made the whole universe by speaking his word. Now he was giving this broken universe and every broken, wandering heart in it the chance to be made new again through that same word—through Jesus, the "Word made flesh," dwelling right here among us.

Based on Luke 2:1-38.

Jesus is baptized by John

Long ago, Joshua had led God's people across the Jordan River to the Promised Land of Canaan. Just as God had done at the Red Sea with Moses, he led his people, creating a path to safety through those waters.

Now, centuries later, another man stood with God's people by the waters of the Jordan River. His name was John.

When people looked at John, they saw a wild man. He wore animal skins and ate locusts and honey. He got their attention!

But that wasn't why people came to the Jordan River to see him. He had an important message to share. Like Isaiah, like Jeremiah, and like Ezekiel, John was a prophet.

John had been a prophet since before his birth. For he was Jesus' cousin. He was the baby who leaped inside his mother, Elizabeth, when Mary visited, pregnant with Jesus. Even though neither child was born yet, he had recognized Mary's baby as the Lord.

Now a grown man, John still knew exactly who Jesus was. For John had come to prepare God's people for the Messiah.

How do we get ready for an important meeting, for a moment that might change us? We get things straight and clean. We put aside anything that isn't important, and we put bad feelings and habits behind us the best we can.

And so John told everyone who would listen, "Repent!"

Like the prophets of earlier times, John gave the people warnings, and he also gave them hope. Standing near the river, near the passage where God had led his people to the Promised Land, John told them of the promised land that would last forever: God's own kingdom.

"Repent!" he preached again and again. "For the kingdom of God is at hand!"

"What shall we do?" the people asked. "How can we get ready?"

John said, "Share what you have. Treat others justly. God is merciful: share his mercy."

And as a sign of God's mercy, of how God can make us clean no matter what we've done, John baptized people there in the river. The Jewish people understood what this meant, for cleansing was an important part of their faith. Before they offered sacrifice or even entered the Temple, they washed themselves.

So when John invited them to welcome God's power into their lives, it made sense: If you were going to cast away darkness, step into the light, and let God change you, you'd begin by letting your whole self be cleansed!

But that wasn't all. John said someone else was coming. "He's mightier than I am," John told them. "I'm baptizing you with water, but he will baptize with the Holy Spirit and with fire."

And one day Jesus came.

Like John, Jesus was a grown man now. He had lived quietly in Nazareth with Mary and Joseph, and his neighbors had called him "the carpenter's son." But now it was time to begin his mission.

So here at the Jordan River, Jesus approached John and asked him to baptize him.

Did Jesus need to repent? Of course not. For Jesus, true God and true man, had never sinned and would never sin. "You should baptize me!" John said to Jesus.

Jesus answered John, "Let it be so now. This is fitting."

Jesus stepped into the waters where John was baptizing God's people, the waters that washed over them as they opened their hearts to God's mercy. He stepped into the river as one of them. He was a human being—a man like us in all things except sin.

As he came up from the waters, the heavens opened. The Spirit of God came down like a dove above his head, and a voice from heaven said,

"This is my beloved Son, with whom I am well pleased."

* * *

After emerging from the waters, Jesus went straight to another place, a place very different from the Jordan's cool, refreshing waters. He went to the dry wilderness of the desert.

Jesus spent forty days in the desert praying, preparing for his mission much as God's people had spent forty years in the desert on their way to the Promised Land, learning, listening, praying, and preparing for their hard mission ahead.

But Jesus wasn't alone in the desert. Because his mission would bring light to the world, darkness wanted it stopped. Darkness would do all it could to shut out the light.

Satan had tempted Eve in the Garden, working on her pride and the hunger to be in charge. And Eve had given in. This was the temptation faced by every human being since then, and it was the temptation Satan used on Jesus as Jesus prayed and fasted in the desert, getting ready.

Jesus was hungry, and so Satan said, "If you're the Son of God, turn these rocks into bread."

Jesus responded with Scripture: "It is written, man shall not live by bread alone, but by every word that proceeds from the mouth of God."

Well then. Satan took Jesus to a high place at the top of a wall surrounding the Temple and tempted him again. "Throw yourself down from here—for it is written that the angels will rescue you."

Jesus answered with more Scripture. "You shall not tempt the Lord your God."

A third time, Satan spoke to him. He took Jesus to a high mountain and showed him all the kingdoms of the world. "I'll give you all of this," he said, "if you worship me."

"Begone, Satan!" Jesus said, "It is written, you shall worship the Lord your God and him only shall you serve!"

With that, the devil was defeated and disappeared, and angels came to feed Jesus.

Now it was time for Jesus to begin his mission. It was time for him to leave the desert and bring the people the Good News their hearts were longing for.

Based on Luke 3–4:1 and Matthew 3–4:1

Jesus calls disciples to a new way of life

After his baptism

and his forty days in the desert, it was time for Jesus to share the Good News of the kingdom of God.

And so he set out. He preached. He taught. He healed. Jesus walked across the land and up and down it, telling people about that kingdom, inviting them to give their whole hearts to God and live with him forever.

But Jesus didn't walk alone. All along the way, friends and helpers walked with him.

It began on the shore of a lake near Jesus' home. This lake was so big, they called it a sea, the Sea of Galilee. Not long after Jesus began his public ministry, he saw two brothers named Simon and Andrew fishing on this lake. He invited the brothers to come and follow him. They dropped their nets right away and came with Jesus.

Soon after, Jesus invited two more brothers, James and John, to join him. More followed until there was a group of them: the Twelve.

These twelve disciples are the ones we call the apostles. They would be Jesus' main students and helpers and his closest friends. Along the way, they were joined by many more disciples.

They were with Jesus as he healed sick people and raised some from the dead. And they were with him as he pulled the lame to their feet, as he touched the ears of the deaf so they could hear again, and as he made mud from his spit and some dirt on the ground and rubbed it on the eyes of a blind man so he could see. Jesus healed the suffering because he loved them and because they had faith in his power. But these healings were also signs. They were signs of what life would be like in heaven: when God reigns, we are whole, and we don't suffer anymore.

The disciples heard him tell parables, or stories. In these parables, Jesus used the things people do in ordinary life—like planting and harvesting, and building or cleaning a house—to help people understand who God is, what God's kingdom is like, and how we can find happiness with him.

Crowds gathered around Jesus wherever he went, and he taught them about the Father's love and mercy. He taught them about what was most important in life and how to find the greatest treasure of all: eternal life with God in his kingdom.

One day, Jesus went up on a hillside to teach. Hills and mountains were very special to God's people. They remembered the times other teachers and prophets had met the Lord in high places. They especially remembered Moses, who had met the Lord on Mount Sinai, surrounded by clouds, lightning, and thunder. And they remembered that when Moses came down from the mountain, he carried with him the Law: the gift from God to his people to guide them to live happy, good lives. He came down from the mountain with the news of a covenant: God would save and protect them, and they would obey him.

Now Jesus stood on another mountain and called them to a new way of life, speaking of the new law that would mark the New Covenant. He had not come to throw away the Law of Moses, he said, but to build on it and fulfill it. He spoke to the people as God had spoken through Moses, about their actions but most of all about transforming the place where our actions begin: our hearts.

"Blessed are the poor in spirit, for theirs is the kingdom of heaven.

Blessed are those who mourn, for they shall be comforted.

Blessed are the meek, for they shall inherit the earth.

Blessed are those who hunger and thirst for righteousness, for they shall be satisfied.

Blessed are the merciful, for they shall obtain mercy.

Blessed are the pure in heart,
for they shall see God.

Blessed are the peacemakers, for
they shall be called sons of God.

Blessed are those who are
persecuted for righteousness' sake,
for theirs is the kingdom of heaven.

Blessed are you when men revile you
and persecute you and utter all kinds
of evil against you falsely on my account.
Rejoice and be glad, for your reward
is great in heaven."

We call this lesson of Jesus the Beatitudes, which comes from a word that means "happy" or "fortunate."

Jesus also spoke to the people about sin. He reminded them of God's Law, given to them from the beginning, but he called them to look not just at what they were doing but at what they were thinking and feeling, too. Anger, greed, and revenge don't begin outside us, Jesus said; they begin on the inside.

Stop judging others, he said. Pray, fast, and give to the poor just as the Law commands—but do it in secret. Don't tell anyone that you are doing good. Only God needs to know, and he already does.

The Law God gave the people through Moses commanded them to love and care for others. Jesus threw the door open and, in this Sermon on the Mount, led God's people to the place the prophets had hinted at, a place where God reigns over a happy, peaceful feast for all the peoples of the world. The way to this place is through love: a love not only for those who are like us and care for us but also for our enemies. Even people who don't believe in God treat their friends well. Jesus asks us to do more. In the New Covenant, we are to love and pray for everyone—even those who hurt us.

Over centuries, God's people were strengthened by the Law and the covenant. They had come to understand who they were and who God called them to be. They had grown in wisdom, coming closer to God's merciful heart. Now Jesus, the Lord himself, was bringing them closer still. From the mount, he was leading them on a journey of their hearts into the Lord's heart, to the eternal promised land of the kingdom of God.

*Based on Matthew 5–7
and Luke 6:20-46.*

Jesus turns water to wine

Jesus preached and taught.
Jesus spoke to people about the Father's mercy. He told parables. He walked dusty roads, rode in boats across lakes, and listened.

Jesus was also a friend. He was also part of a family. He spent time with his family and friends. He gathered with them, shared meals, and traveled with them.

One day, Mary, Jesus, and his disciples went to a party.

It was the celebration of a wedding feast, and it was happening in the town of Cana in Galilee, the same area in northern Israel where Jesus grew up. During Jesus' time, wedding celebrations went on for several days, sometimes even a week. The bride and groom were surrounded by their parents, brothers, sisters, cousins, aunts and uncles, and lots of friends, eating, laughing, singing, and drinking.

At one point during the feast, Mary noticed something: the party had run out of wine! This was a problem. Of course it was a problem because no one wants to run out of wine during their wedding feast. But running out of wine would also be embarrassing for the family hosting the party.

So Mary found Jesus and told him about the problem. Jesus answered at first, "Why are you telling me this? My hour has not yet come." Mary then hurried to the servants and told them, "Do whatever he tells you."

Jesus told the servants to get the six stone jars that stood nearby, huge jars that usually held the water used for purification before worship. And he told them to fill those jars with water.

The servants obeyed. The jars each held twenty or thirty gallons of water, and the servants filled each to the brim.

Now, Jesus said, take a cup, draw some out, and take that cup to the man in charge of the feast. They did, and when the man took a drink, he was surprised. It wasn't water—it was wine! And more than that: it was a very fine wine! So he went to the bridegroom and asked him why he'd saved the best wine for last.

He said, "Usually at parties, people serve the best wine first, so that partygoers won't notice the poor wine they're drinking later. Why did you save the good wine until now?"

It was a miracle indeed for Jesus to turn all that water into the finest wine. Seeing it, his disciples believed in him.

The apostle John, who tells us about this miracle in his Gospel, calls this the first of Jesus' signs. What is a sign? It is something that points us to something else, something meaningful and big. Jesus' miracles are signs because they help us see something important. Through them Jesus shows us what the kingdom of God is like.

When Jesus heals lepers, gives sight to the blind, and helps the lame walk, he is showing us that God's kingdom is a place of wholeness and health. When Jesus calms a storm, he shows us that in his kingdom God indeed reigns over all people and all things—even the mightiest storms.

When Jesus turns the water into wine, it is also a sign. It is a sign of what the Lord wants to give us when we say yes to him, when we do what he tells us—a sign of God's overflowing bounty. And it is a sign of something else, as well. It is a sign that points to Jesus himself.

Remember, these weren't just any old jars that Jesus had filled with water. They were jars, carved from a single chunk of stone, that were used in religious ceremonies. They were special, and the water in them was special, used in worship and ritual.

When Jesus turned the water in these special jars into an abundance of wine, it was a sign that God has abundant goodness to share with his people—and it would come through Jesus. Water was good. Water could quench our thirst and clean us. But through wine—like the cup of wine at the Last Supper—Jesus would give us his very self. Jesus would give us life, and life in abundance.

And who was it who helped this happen? Mary, of course!

Mary noticed that people were in need, and she went right to Jesus, asking him to help. When we are in trouble or in need, we can always pray to Jesus. But just as we ask others to help us with hard things on earth, so we can also ask all the saints, and especially Mary, to help us from heaven. We send our prayers to Mary and the saints, asking them to intercede for us, asking her to help us through her prayers, just as she helped at Cana.

And we hear Mary speaking to us in the same words she said to the servants at Cana. We trust Jesus, we trust in the abundant life he promises us and in the miracles and signs he gives us. And we hear Mary's words in our hearts, guiding us to that place of happiness and joy, just as she guided those servants:

"Do whatever he tells you."

Based on John 2:1-12.

Jesus names **Peter** to lead the **Church**

Jesus had been preaching, teaching, healing, and forgiving for some time. One day, Jesus and his friends arrived at a town called Caesarea Philippi. Remember that the whole region was under the control of the Roman Empire now. Caesarea Philippi had even more importance: here Herod, the ruler of Judea, had built a pagan temple in honor of the Roman emperor Caesar Augustus.

Jesus brought his friends to this place where pagan gods and earthly men were honored, and he asked them a question: "Who do men say I am?"

So many people had been listening to Jesus preach and teach. They'd witnessed his healings. What, Jesus asked, were they saying about him?

His apostles told him that some were saying he was John the Baptist, even though by this time John had been killed by Herod. Maybe John had come back to life? The apostles also told Jesus that some were saying he might be one of the prophets. Maybe he was Elijah, the prophet the Jewish people believed would come back again before the Messiah. Or maybe he was Jeremiah, another great prophet.

Now Jesus had another question. Not about the crowds but about his friends, who'd been on the journey with him, who'd listened to him carefully and seen his power.

"Who do *you* say that I am?"

One of his very first followers spoke up quickly. It was Simon. He said, "You are the Christ, the Son of the living God."

When Simon said this, he showed that he understood. He knew who Jesus was. Simon knew that Jesus was much more than just a man, more even than a special prophet. Simon called Jesus "the Christ," which means the Messiah—the Savior God's people had been waiting for. He also called Jesus the Son of God!

Jesus told him that this deep understanding of the truth came from God.

In the Bible, when God chooses someone for a special task, he often changes that person's name: Abram became Abraham, Jacob became Israel. And now, Jesus said, Simon would have a new name: Jesus told him that now he would be known as Peter.

In Greek, the word for *Peter* means "rock." Now, in Caesarea Philippi, standing near a rock where pagan people worshipped earthly powers and false idols, Jesus told Simon Peter that he was the "rock" on which Jesus would build his Church. He told Peter that this Church would be stronger than death and darkness. He told him that now Peter would hold keys to the kingdom of heaven. Whatever Peter bound on earth would be bound in heaven, too.

Peter would be the earthly leader of the new community of believers that Jesus was building: the Church. This community would continue the work that the apostles had seen Jesus accomplish on earth. The Church, led by the bishops and the pope, succeeding the apostles and Peter, would continue to teach and guide and forgive sins in Jesus' name, doing just what Jesus had shown them—to the ends of the earth.

Simon Peter's answer had been true and good. But did Jesus' friends really understand? There was a great mystery still. For God's people had expected a messiah, or savior, who would free them from earthly troubles—who would even, perhaps, in this moment help them throw off the chains of the Roman Empire and make them free again, as they were under King David's reign. They expected a messiah who would lead them to worldly glory once again.

But was this what Jesus meant? His friends had to wonder. For soon after Jesus pointed to Simon Peter as the rock who would lead God's people, he immediately spoke of King David's own city of Jerusalem, saying it was time for them to go there. And there, he told them, he would suffer—and be killed!

This was confusing. It was not what anyone, even the disciples, expected from the long-awaited Messiah. Martyrdom? It couldn't be! The Messiah was supposed to come in glory, defeat God's enemies, and

lead God's people to the glory they'd enjoyed with King David. Peter protested. He told Jesus that it couldn't happen—Jesus couldn't go there to suffer and die!

Jesus had strong words for Peter then. "Get behind me!" he told him. Peter still didn't understand. It would take time for him and for all Jesus' friends to see what Jesus, the Son of the Living God, was saving them from and leading them toward.

God had called his people into a covenant through Abraham and Moses. That covenant was lived out by the twelve tribes of Israel following God's covenant Law written on tablets of stone. Now, through Jesus the Messiah, God was calling his people into a new covenant, written in their hearts, guided by the twelve apostles, solid and sure, and led by Peter, the rock.

Based on Matthew 16:13-20.

Jesus is transfigured on a mountaintop

We can be close to God

wherever we are. But there are special places where we can be especially close to God. So when God spoke to Moses from the burning bush, he told him to take off his shoes, since in that special place, Moses was standing on holy ground.

Mountains and other high places have always been special spots where God's people have met and come close to the Lord, who created and reigns over the whole world spread around us.

It was on a mountain that the prophet Elijah heard the quiet voice of God whispering to him. It was on a mountain that Moses spent forty days close to the Lord, surrounded by lightning and thunder, receiving the Law and covenant. It is on a mountain in the heights of heaven, Isaiah writes, that God will one day gather his people, those who say yes to his love and mercy, to feast and celebrate together forever. And it was on a hillside in Galilee that Jesus shared the Beatitudes, the heart of the New Covenant, with God's people.

And so Jesus took his closest friends to Mount Tabor in Galilee to pray. Up the mountain they walked, Jesus with Peter and the brothers James and John. When they reached the top, there was no thunder or lightning. There were no trumpets blasting. There was no storm.

But as Jesus began to pray, there was light.

So much light! The light came from Jesus himself. His face shone like the sun, and his garments became a dazzling white. He was transfigured before them, still himself, still Jesus, but radiant, so much more glorious than they had understood before.

And they found that they weren't alone. For with them on the mountain were both Moses and Elijah. These two men, who had met the Lord on mountains before in their earthly lives, were here now on this mountain, talking to Jesus. They spoke of just what Jesus had told his friends earlier: of how the Lord would suffer in Jerusalem and all that he would do there.

Though Peter and the others were heavy with sleep, Peter saw the great men of the past speaking with Jesus, his friend and teacher, and he didn't want to forget this place and time.

Over the centuries, the Lord met his people in many special and amazing ways. He led them through deserts and through rushing waters. He gave them the Law and shared the covenant with them. He promised them life, love, and a home. He forgave them over and over.

And his people responded with their lives and their gratitude but also with signs and symbols to mark the holy places where God had met them here on earth. They said special prayers, wore special garments, built altars of stones and the glorious Temple.

This was no different. Thinking perhaps of the Feast of Booths that God's people celebrated to remember the Exodus, Peter said to Jesus, "It's good that we are here! Let us build three booths here—one for you, one for Moses, and one for Elijah!"

At that very moment, a cloud came—not a dark cloud but a bright, shining one. Afraid, Peter, James, and John listened as a voice came from the cloud—the same voice that was heard at Jesus' baptism. It said, "This is my beloved Son, with whom I am well pleased. Listen to him!"

And the disciples fell down in awe. There on the mountaintop, the Holy Trinity—Father, Son, and Holy Spirit—revealed to them who Jesus was. It was just as Peter had said: Jesus was indeed the Messiah, the Son of the Living God.

Then the cloud disappeared, and Moses and Elijah disappeared, and Jesus touched the disciples and told them gently to get up. Things were as before, and it was time for them to leave the mountaintop.

The apostles had seen and heard a great, beautiful mystery. But they couldn't build booths and stay there forever. They stood and turned back to the path that would take them to Jerusalem. Hard times lay ahead, just as Jesus had said. But the Lord had given them a gift, too, up high on that mountain. He'd given them a glimpse of his glory, the glory awaiting him at the end of that dusty, hard road to Jerusalem.

Based on Luke 9:28-36.

Jesus offers his Body and Blood

Jesus and his friends

had traveled around the land, north to south and east to west. In villages, on hillsides, and on the shores of lakes and rivers, Jesus shared the Good News: the kingdom of God was at hand!

God had created and formed his people over the centuries. Now he was inviting them to come even closer to him. He was calling them to know his mercy and love, and to hear it in a human voice and to be touched by it with human hands: his hands. The hands of Jesus, the Son of God, the "Word made flesh" dwelling among them. The kingdom of God was among them!

Women and men, boys and girls heard Jesus and responded to him. They were healed. They were forgiven and changed their lives. But not everyone liked what they saw and heard. Some people just didn't understand. Some stopped listening because he called them to a different and in some ways harder life. And some religious leaders were threatened and angered by Jesus. Who was he to say that people's sins were forgiven? Who was he to pick grain or heal on the Sabbath, the day of rest? Who did he think he was? God?

Over one short week, all of these strong feelings about Jesus came to life—and it all happened in Jerusalem.

The week began with great joy. It was the week before Passover—the feast celebrating the Jewish people's escape from slavery in Egypt—and as with all the great feasts, many people were traveling to Jerusalem to celebrate. Among those crowds were Jesus and his friends.

As people heard of his coming, they gathered. News about Jesus had spread. People were talking about him, and many wanted to see him and touch him and hear him teach. Many had decided that this man, the "son of Joseph the carpenter," just might be the Messiah, come to save them!

Jesus entered Jerusalem that day riding on a donkey. And the people greeted him with joy, crowding around him, waving palms, spreading them out before him, and singing the ancient psalms of David: Hosanna! Blessed is the one who comes in the name of the Lord!

After this happy beginning, the days passed, and the time came to celebrate the Passover meal. Jesus and his friends gathered in the upper room of a house to share the same meal that God's people had been sharing since the time of Moses. At the Passover meal, a family would eat special foods: bitter herbs to remind

them of their hard lives in Egypt; lamb to remind them of the lambs' blood spread on their doorposts to save them from the angel of death; unleavened bread as a remembrance of the speed with which they had left Egypt; and several cups of wine. But this meal was different, for Jesus himself is the Passover Lamb.

Before the meal began, Jesus, as he always did, was leading the disciples to a deeper place in the heart of God.

In those days, if a person wore shoes, they were probably sandals, and walking on those dusty roads, a person's feet would get very dirty during the day. When you wanted to settle down and enjoy time with family and friends indoors, you'd want to be as clean as possible, of course, and not bring that dust inside. So washing feet was a normal, everyday task.

It was also usually a task for servants and slaves. Hosts didn't wash their guests' feet. Guests didn't wash each other's feet.

But that night, Jesus knelt down and washed the feet of each of his friends.

Peter had something to say! He did not want Jesus to wash his feet, just as Jesus' cousin John had said Jesus should be baptizing him, not the other way around.

No, Jesus said, this is what he had to do. And if he, their master and teacher, washed their feet, they would see that this is what they were to do for each other: serve, in love and sacrifice.

It was time for the Passover meal. As always, it was a meal of prayer and remembrance. The apostles were used to thinking of this meal as a way of remembering their ancestors' flight from Egypt, God acting with strength, defeating the powers of death. It was as if they were with them again on the journey out of slavery.

But as Jesus took up the unleavened bread in his hands, the prayer and remembrance were transformed.

Jesus held the unleavened bread in his hands.

"This is my body," he said, "which is given for you. Do this in remembrance of me."

Then he took up the chalice, the cup of wine.

"This chalice which is poured out for you is the new covenant in my blood."

The apostles didn't know what was going to happen the next day. But Jesus did—he had told them about the suffering that was about to come. In the Passover meal, God's people celebrated their freedom. Now Jesus, through the food that was his Body and his Blood, was leading them in an even deeper way of freedom.

He was the Lamb of God, and his life would be given so we could be free from the most hurtful chains of all: sin and death.

This Passover meal joined Jesus' friends in a New Covenant with God. It is the covenant in which God pours out his life for us and into us. It is a covenant that gives life, not just on earth but forever in heaven. Jesus promised that whenever they gathered to share this bread and wine of the New Covenant—his Body and Blood—he would be with them.

But just as before, from the Garden of Eden until now, no matter how much love and mercy God pours out, human beings are tempted to step away, take another path, and listen to another voice.

"This very night," Jesus said, "one of you will betray me."

And he went out into the night, to the Mount of Olives, to pray. And his disciples followed him.

Based on Luke 22:7-39 and John 13:3-8.

Jesus is condemned to death

Deep in the night, in a garden called Gethsemane, Jesus prayed.

He asked Peter and the other disciples to stay awake and pray with him, but they didn't. One by one, they fell asleep, and Jesus was left alone with the Father in prayer.

"Father," he prayed, "if you are willing, remove this chalice from me; nevertheless, not my will, but yours be done." Jesus knew what awaited him. He knew the forces that were getting ready to battle him. He knew he would suffer, and he had told the disciples.

But still they slept.

As he prayed, angels came to help and comfort him, and still he prayed so hard and so deeply that the sweat on his brow turned to blood.

The disciples slept on.

All, that is, except one, who had slipped away from the rest of them. Wide awake and on the move, his name was Judas, and he went to the religious leaders who he knew didn't like Jesus and were afraid of him. Judas had offered to tell them where Jesus was in exchange for money—thirty pieces of silver.

And so they arrived—Judas, the religious leaders, and soldiers. Judas greeted Jesus, as was the custom, with a kiss. "Judas," Jesus asked, "would you betray the Son of Man with a kiss?"

The answer, of course, was yes. Judas had betrayed Jesus and turned him over to the religious and government powers that would work together to bring his earthly life, his ministry of love and mercy, to, they hoped, an end.

They took Jesus to Caiaphas, the high priest at the Temple there in Jerusalem. Caiaphas was opposed to Jesus because of what Jesus said about himself and God the Father. Jesus forgave sins, which only God can do. Jesus had referred to himself as "I AM," the name the Lord revealed to Moses in the burning bush. Jesus had spoken of himself as sitting at God's right hand, in a place of honor and authority.

Caiaphas and the other religious leaders didn't understand how Jesus could say these things and still think of himself as a good and faithful religious person. What Jesus said was, they believed, blasphemy, a terrible sin.

So Caiaphas asked Jesus, brought before him as a prisoner, "Are you the Son of God?"

Jesus answered, "You say that I am."

That was enough for Caiaphas and the other religious leaders. They wanted Jesus gone. So they sent Jesus to the Roman governor, Pilate, who was in charge of punishing those who made trouble in that part of the Roman Empire. But first, Caiaphas' guards mocked Jesus and beat him. They tied a cloth over his eyes and jeered at him.

"Prophesy!" they said. "Who is it that struck you?"

When Jesus was taken to Caiaphas, Peter followed. As Peter waited outside, a servant girl asked him if he was one of Jesus' disciples, but he said he wasn't. Two more times he was asked if he knew Jesus, and two more times he said no. When he realized what he had done— three times he denied the Lord—he went away and wept bitterly.

The religious leaders told Pilate that Jesus had been saying he was a king, a challenger to Caesar. Pilate asked Jesus if he was the king of the Jews. Jesus simply answered, "You have said so."

Pilate couldn't find any serious threat in Jesus. But the religious leaders insisted that he was a troublemaker. Well, said Pilate, let Herod deal with him then.

Now Herod was a king—but not a king with any real power. He did whatever the Roman leaders thought was best. Herod was curious about Jesus and his miracles, for he'd heard a lot about him. But when Herod asked him questions, Jesus remained silent. So Herod and his soldiers also mocked him and sent him back to Pilate.

Meanwhile, angry crowds were gathering outside. The people who had celebrated

Jesus when he entered Jerusalem started to turn on him.

Pilate announced that he didn't see any reason to punish Jesus anymore and offered to release him, for it was a custom around Passover time to give a prisoner his freedom.

But the people didn't want him to be released.

"Barabbas!" they cried. Barabbas was a man imprisoned for rebelling against the Roman Empire. "Give us Barabbas!" they cried.

Pilate asked the crowd if they were sure. Yes, they cried. Three times he asked. "Crucify him!" they shouted.

Pilate washed his hands. He said it wasn't his problem anymore. Jesus was condemned.

Now Jesus was taken by the Roman soldiers to a courtyard where they tied him to a pillar and whipped him. Then they, too, mocked him, dressing him up like a pretend king and pushing a crown of sharp thorns hard onto his head.

How was he to be killed? By the punishment the Romans used for the worst criminals of all, for those they wanted to humiliate and use as examples and warnings: crucifixion.

Jesus had to carry part of his own cross to his own crucifixion, and so he did, surrounded by the crowds. The journey led through the narrow streets of the city

that had welcomed him as a king, the hoped-for Messiah, just days before. Now he stumbled on, bearing the burden of the sins of the world.

Some jeered at him, but others wept. Jesus gave comfort to those who were sad, and he accepted comfort from those who gave it—people like Simon of Cyrene, who helped Jesus carry his cross.

On he walked, until he reached a hill called Golgotha, which means "place of a skull," outside the city walls. Just a few hours before, Jesus had spoken to his friends of love and sacrifice. He had told them there was no greater love than for a man to lay down his life for his friends. He had shared bread and wine with them and also a great mystery: that in that meal, in that moment, they were sharing his very life, which was being poured out for them in the New Covenant.

It was a Friday. Under the noonday sun, the soldiers stripped the prisoner and prepared the wood of the Cross.

Based on Luke 22:39–23:43.

Jesus is crucified

God created a beautiful world.
He created women and men in his own
image. He looked at every bit of it and
called it good. He created it all out of
love and through his word.

But over and over, his children turned
from him. And over and over, the Lord
forgave them and guided them. He
showed them the way to live that would
bring happiness and wholeness to the
world and to each person in it.

Still, they turned away.

When it was time, then, in the fullness
of time, God entered the world in the
most special way possible: He came as
one of us. He came as the "Word made
flesh," the Son of God, Jesus, born of
Mary, who walked with us, talked with
us, taught, and preached. He came
among us so we could hear God's
voice and know God's touch.

And he came to give us the greatest
gift of all: forgiveness. For long ago,
in the Garden, Adam and Eve had

turned away from their Creator and said no to his gift. They sinned, and their children and their children's children sinned as well. They turned away from life and met instead darkness and death. How could this ever end?

It would end in the same way it began: with a gift. God gave his creation the gift of life, and now, as Jesus said yes to God's will in another garden, the gift of eternal life would be ours once again. But to meet darkness and death, to win that victory over sin? That wasn't an easy path.

Now, at Golgotha, Jesus, who had walked among the people sharing nothing but love and truth, hung on a cross.

How had he gotten there? Sin had taken him to that place. Not his own sin, of course, but the sins of the world, sin that had selfishly turned away, sin that had been afraid and proud, sin that had declared that human beings have power over life and death, the power that only God possesses.

And Jesus, without sin himself, had accepted it, borne the scourging and beatings, been humiliated and struck down, and was now nailed and raised on a cross, as the sun beat down and voices were raised to mock him again.

The voices came from all sides. They came from the soldiers who gambled for his garments, telling him to save himself since he'd saved so many others.

They came from a fellow prisoner. On either side of him were two thieves, also condemned by the Romans, nailed to their own crosses. One of them made fun of him, angry and suffering himself. "Are you not the Christ? Save yourself and us!" he cried.

But the other thief scolded him. "Don't you fear God?" he said. "We deserve our punishment—but this man was innocent. He didn't do anything wrong." And then he begged Jesus, "When you come into your kingdom, remember me." And Jesus, suffering there on the Cross, assured him, "Today you will be with me in paradise."

The apostles had almost all fled, including Peter, who had denied knowing him three times on the night Jesus was arrested.

But three people remained at the foot of the Cross. John was the young apostle who later wrote his memories of Jesus in a Gospel. Mary of Magdala had once been possessed by terrible demons, which Jesus drove out. And with them, of course, was Jesus' mother.

Mary stood at the foot of the Cross. She wouldn't leave her son. Before his birth, the angel had said he would save Israel.

Now Mary stayed with him through all that terrible afternoon.

Jesus, looking down from the Cross, saw her, and he saw John.

He told Mary, "Behold your son."

He told John, "Behold your mother."

He gave them to each other. He gave Mary, his own mother, to the apostle John—not only to care for her, but as a sign to the whole Church. She is our mother, too.

The afternoon wore on. Nailed to the Cross, Jesus suffered greatly, as the prophet Isaiah had said God's servant would.

At last Jesus said, "I thirst." And in response, still mocking him, someone gave him bitter vinegar to drink.

It was three o'clock in the afternoon.

"It is finished," he said. And Jesus died.

Now the soldiers broke the legs of the two criminals on either side of Jesus. But they didn't break Jesus' legs. Instead, a soldier pierced his side with a lance, and from the wound blood and water flowed out. From that they knew that he had died, and it was time to take him down from the Cross.

In the quiet sadness of that late afternoon, a man named Joseph of Arimathea got Pilate's permission to place Jesus' body in a tomb he owned. The tomb, carved out of rock, was in a garden close by, and it had never been used. In these days and in this place, people weren't buried in the ground. They were generally laid in tombs above ground, either in heavy stone coffins, beautifully carved, or in caves sealed up with stones.

It was almost evening, when the Sabbath would begin. Joseph of Arimathea and the women who had stayed with Jesus took Jesus' body down from the Cross, wrapped it in linen cloths, and laid it in the tomb. And the women saw the heavy stone rolled across the opening, and in those sad moments, they said goodbye.

Based on Luke 23:50-56 and John 19:25-42.

Jesus rises
from the dead

Mary Magdalene was on her way to Jesus' tomb. It was the third day after Jesus died on the Cross, and she and her friends had work to do.

In those days, friends and family took tender care of the bodies of their loved ones who had died. They cleaned the bodies themselves, wrapped them in burial cloths, and anointed them with oils and herbs. Mary, another woman named Mary (not Jesus' mother), and Salome had begun the work on Friday, but since the Sabbath began that evening and work was forbidden on the day of rest, they couldn't finish.

So now, on the morning of a new day and the first day after the Sabbath, the women returned. They had all been friends and followers of Jesus, walking alongside him on his journeys through Israel, listening to him, witnessing his mighty deeds, and at the end, accompanying him as far as they could on his journey to Golgotha.

They had seen him die on the Cross. They had helped take down his body and lay it in the tomb two days before. They had seen the tomb sealed with a large, heavy stone. As far as they knew, it was the end of that journey. Wasn't it always that way when someone died?

But this morning, as they came close to the tomb, carved in the rocky hillside, they noticed something very, very strange.

The stone that had been used to seal the tomb had been rolled away!

Looking inside, the women saw something even stranger: the tomb was empty!

While they were wondering what in the world was going on, two men, dazzling with bright light, stood by them.

"Why," they asked, "do you seek the living among the dead? He is not here. He is risen."

Then the men reminded the women of all that Jesus had told them before. He had told them that he would suffer and be handed over to be crucified. All that had happened. But what else had he told them? He had, indeed, told them that on the third day … he would rise!

The women remembered this, and then, of course, they rushed to do what any of us would do—spread this amazing good news!

They found the apostles, who had left Jesus during his passion. They told Peter and Jesus' other friends what they'd seen—but it was just too strange. Surely they were imagining things. The apostles didn't believe them, and Peter ran to see for himself.

Sure enough, as he entered the tomb, he saw exactly what the women had described: It was empty, and the burial cloths were just lying there on the stone slab. Jesus' body was gone, nowhere to be seen. What had happened? Peter wondered. Where was the Lord?

Back in the beginning of time, God had set about his work of Creation. At the very end, with the last words of Creation, God had made woman and man, our first parents, and given them a life of beauty, peace, and harmony in the Garden of Eden. He had created them out of love, spoken them into existence through his word, and breathed his own life into them.

On the last day, he had looked around at all he had made and declared it to be very good. And on that seventh day, he had rested.

Now it was the first day of the week. It was the first day in a different garden, a place once rocky and sad but now alive with new life. It was the first day of a new creation, the gift of eternal life with Jesus, the "Word made flesh," the Son of God, victorious over sin and death, risen from the dead. The sin committed in Eden had been reconciled, the death of that disobedience conquered by the obedience of the Son of God.

God's Creation at the beginning of time was a gift. It was a gift of life and love, poured out in unbelievable variety, beauty, and order, from tiny atoms to the magnificent stars in the sky. And so on the first day of the new creation, the gift of new life is poured out, eternal life and reconciliation between human beings and God … if we choose to listen and follow and say yes to the one who says,

I am the way, the truth, and the life.

Based on Luke 24:1-12.

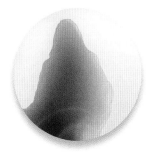

Jesus appears to disciples; later **ascends** into heaven

For forty days,
Jesus walked, talked, and shared meals again with his friends.

He was the same Jesus they had known before the Crucifixion. They recognized his face and his voice. They ate with him; they touched his wounds. But there was something new about his presence with them as well.

The first to meet Jesus that first day was Mary Magdalene. She had returned to the garden where Jesus' tomb was, wondering where his body was, when a man approached her. She thought it was a gardener, and she asked him what had been done with Jesus' body. But then that man said her name, "Mary!" And she recognized him immediately—it was the Lord!

Later that day, two disciples were walking from Jerusalem to the small town of Emmaus, talking about all that had happened. A man met them in the road and asked what they were discussing. They said, "Are you the only one who hasn't heard?" So as they walked, they told the man about Jesus

263

and his crucifixion. When they arrived at Emmaus, the disciples invited the man to share a meal with them. He did, and when the man picked up bread and broke it to share, immediately the disciples recognized him—it was Jesus!

These two disciples rushed to tell the others what they'd seen, and that very evening, Jesus appeared among them again! "Peace be with you!" Jesus said to them, for they were, of course, confused and a little frightened. "Why are you troubled?" he asked, and he showed them the wounds on his hands and his feet—it was really Jesus.

He was really alive—he wasn't a ghost or a spirit. They could see the wounds, and they even watched him eat—for he asked them for a piece of grilled fish and ate it right there in front of them.

It was really and truly Jesus. They knew him, and they could touch him. But he would come to them in surprising ways, and they didn't always recognize him at first. He was the same, but there was a mystery about his presence as well.

All of this was hard to believe and understand. Even though Jesus had told the apostles that he would suffer and die and even though he had promised that he would rise again, no one had ever seen anything like that before. The apostle

Thomas heard what the others were saying, but doubted. "I won't believe," he said, "until I touch his wounds."

Later, the apostles were gathered in a room with the doors tightly shut when Jesus came to them. "Peace be with you," he said. He then turned to Thomas and told him, "Put your finger here, and see my hands. Put out your hand, and place it in my side."

Thomas did. He touched the wounds of the living Jesus, whom he'd last seen condemned to die. "My Lord and my God!" he exclaimed.

And so Jesus stayed with his friends, teaching and guiding them for those forty days. He wasn't doing this just for their sake. Jesus hadn't come to earth to save just a small group of friends or a certain number of people. One day he met them on a mountain in Galilee, and he made this clear to them: What he had given them was for everyone. He was giving them the authority to share this Good News right from his word, his heart, his suffering, and his risen life:

"Go out to the whole world," he told them. "Make disciples of all nations. Baptize them in the name of the Father, the Son, and the Holy Spirit. Teach them to live as I've taught you. I will be with you until the end of the age."

He would be with them as he promised, but it would be in a different way than they had known. For if they were to go through the whole world sharing the Good News, how could Jesus be with each of them, everywhere, all the time?

The apostles gathered with Jesus on earth one last time in Bethany. They asked him if it was time for him to restore the kingdom of Israel then. Jesus answered that it wasn't for anyone on earth to know the day or the hour or how exactly God's plan would be worked out. But over the years, during every time and season, they could be at peace. The Holy Spirit was going to be given to them. With this Holy Spirit, they would have the gifts of wisdom and courage, and they would speak and minister with the Lord's own authority.

Jesus would continue to work through them—through their words, their healing touch, their sharing, their acts of love, kindness, and mercy. His presence—his body—would remain on earth: through them.

And then, in a moment, Jesus was raised up. As the apostles watched, he was lifted up, and a cloud surrounded him and took him away.

As the apostles stood and studied the heavens, watching where Jesus had gone, two men came and stood with them. "Men of Galilee," they asked, "why do you stand looking into heaven?" Jesus, they said, would return someday.

In the meantime, as he promised, he stayed with his friends in a new way. He would be everywhere, whenever his friends gathered to pray. He would continue to act through them just as he promised: forgiving sins, sharing mercy, bringing young and old into the embrace of eternal life through Baptism, and feeding their very souls with himself, the Bread of Life.

He would remain on earth through his Church.

Based on Matthew 28:18-20, Luke 24:36-53, and Acts 1:1-14.

THE CHURCH
TIME PERIOD

AD 33 to the present

The Holy Spirit descends on the followers of
Jesus, filling them with wisdom and strength.
The apostles and disciples boldly proclaim the
gospel to all who will listen, and Christianity
spreads to the Gentiles and to many nations.
Under the leadership of Peter, the Church
begins its mission, which continues to this day.

The Holy Spirit descends on Mary and the apostles

Ten days had passed
since Jesus ascended into heaven.

The apostles spent those ten days in Jerusalem, the place where Jesus had been condemned and crucified—ten days in the city where the religious leaders still looked at Jesus' friends with suspicion.

Yes, Jesus had told them to go out to the whole world and share the Good News. He had told them to baptize all people.

He had told them he'd be with them and the Holy Spirit would give them strength and wisdom.

They'd heard Jesus say all this. They'd seen Jesus keep his promises over and over again. But it had been only two months since they'd seen Jesus arrested and killed. They knew Jesus was alive, but it was an amazing story that was hard to believe. Who knows how those religious leaders and the Roman authorities would react if they just went out and started talking about it? Would the apostles be the next ones to be crucified?

And so they gathered in a room and they prayed. For nine days, they prayed together, waiting.

Then on the tenth day, fifty days after Jesus rose from the dead, as the apostles and Jesus' mother, Mary, were praying in that room in Jerusalem, something happened.

A sound rushed through the room. It was the sound of a great, strong, mighty wind.

They saw tongues of flames—like little fires being lit over the heads of Mary and each apostle. Flames burning bright and strong! Just then, they all began to speak, too. They were filled with the Holy Spirit, speaking in all sorts of different languages.

The wind rushed. The fires flickered. The Spirit moved. Filled with the power of the Holy Spirit, they went out into the world to proclaim the Good News!

Jerusalem was a very busy place just then. It was the weeklong feast of Pentecost, the celebration of the Lord giving the Law to Moses on Mount Sinai. As with all important feasts, the people would gather to celebrate this holy day in their holiest city—Jerusalem. They would come from all over the Roman Empire, from the north, south, east, and west, to pray at the Temple, offer sacrifice, and thank God for his gifts.

So even though the apostles were in one place, one city called Jerusalem, that day it was as if the whole world had come to them!

The apostles rushed out into the city, filled with the Spirit and his gifts, just as Jesus had promised. They were filled with understanding, wisdom, and strength. They began to speak, and all those people gathered from all over the world heard them—but each heard them speak in that person's own language!

"Aren't these men from Galilee?" the people wondered. "But we are each hearing them in our own language! We are Parthians, Medes, and Elamites. We are from Mesopotamia, Judea and Cappadocia, Pontus and Asia, Egypt, and even Rome!"

Everyone wondered what this could mean. Some thought it was obviously the work of God, but others laughed, saying that these men, bursting out and speaking so wildly, had been drinking too much that day.

Now Peter stood up, apart from the others. Peter, the fisherman whom Jesus had called to be the rock of his Church, his body on earth, began to speak.

First, he assured the people that the apostles weren't drunk. That wasn't why they spoke this way and could be understood by all. No, it was the power of God! Just as the prophet Joel had said, God had poured out his Spirit. He was sending signs!

When we see a sign, we pay attention. We know something important is ahead. And all of these gifts the Spirit was pouring out on the apostles and making known there in Jerusalem that day were a sign—a sign that pointed back to Jesus himself.

So Peter told the crowd the story of Jesus. He told them that Jesus had been sent by God and had performed mighty signs and wonders. But even though Jesus had done nothing but good, evil men still tried to stop him— and Peter told the crowd the story of Jesus' arrest and crucifixion.

But that, Peter said, wasn't the end of the story.

"God raised him up, having loosed the pangs of death … This Jesus God raised up, and of that we all are witnesses!"

And as the people listened, Peter preached loud and clear: "God has made him both Lord and Christ, this Jesus whom you crucified."

It was, in a way, the Tower of Babel turned around. At Babel, proud human beings were trying to be like God, and he confused their speech. Speaking in different languages, they could no longer understand each other.

But on this new day of Pentecost, God gave his people the gift of understanding once again. They could hear the Good News and, if they put their pride aside and listened in humility to the story of Jesus' love, sacrifice, and mercy, no matter what language they spoke, they would understand. And at last, again, they would be one!

Based on Acts 2:1-41.

Deacons help to spread the gospel

During his time on earth, Jesus had preached, taught, healed, and shared God's mercy. The apostles now understood that this was their job, too. They were the Church, Christ's body on earth, and Jesus had called them, not to live for themselves anymore, but to live in communion with him, letting him work through them to reconcile this broken world to God.

And so it began in Jerusalem. Empowered by the Holy Spirit at Pentecost, no longer afraid, the apostles got to work.

But there was so much work to do! So many people needed and wanted to hear the Good News, to hear the story of Jesus' life, death, and resurrection. But there were also so many people in need! There were hungry and poor people, widows and orphans. The apostles couldn't do it all themselves. They needed help.

Of course, they were joined by many along the way—on the day of Pentecost alone, after Peter's sermon, three thousand people were baptized. But if Jesus' mission was to continue, it had to be organized. So to help the apostles do what Jesus had commanded—preaching and teaching, baptizing, and tending to those in need—the apostles, led by the Holy Spirit, chose helpers.

The Twelve—for they had replaced Judas with a new apostle, Matthias, and were twelve again—called all the Christians in Jerusalem together. Under the guidance of the Holy Spirit, seven men would be called who were full of the Spirit and full of wisdom. These men, called deacons, would have the special task of helping the poor. One of these men was named Philip.

One day, the deacon Philip was on the road. He had been preaching and healing people in Samaria, north of Jerusalem, when an angel of the Lord appeared to him and directed him to return south. Philip obeyed.

Walking on the desert road between Jerusalem and Gaza, Philip saw a beautiful chariot. In the chariot was

an official of the Ethiopian royal court who worked for Candace, that nation's queen. Deep in his heart, Philip felt a nudge and heard a voice. "Go up and join this chariot," the Spirit told him. And so Philip did.

As he approached, he saw and heard the Ethiopian reading—for in those days, most people when they read books or scrolls did not read silently, but aloud. He recognized the words that the man was reading—they were from the Scriptures! So Philip approached and asked the man if he understood what he was reading.

The man answered, "How can I, unless someone guides me?"

And he invited Philip to come up into his chariot with him and explain the words of the prophet. The words the Ethiopian was reading were from the prophet Isaiah: "As a sheep led to the slaughter or a lamb before its shearer is silent, so he opens not his mouth."

That might be hard to understand—unless you knew the story of Jesus. The Ethiopian asked Philip who the prophet was talking about, himself or someone else? It was clear why the Holy Spirit had led Philip to this place, at this very time—to tell the Ethiopian all about Jesus.

So Philip explained. It was Jesus whom the prophets had foretold, the one who would suffer for the sake of the world's sins. He was the one who would suffer patiently and in silence. He was the one whom God would raise in glory, who would sit at God's right hand.

This is what Philip told the Ethiopian— the same story that he had heard from the apostles who had known and seen Jesus themselves. In an unbroken chain, the Good News was shared once again.

As they rode along, they came to a body of water, and there, having listened to all Philip had to say, the Ethiopian was ready. "Here is some water," he said. "What is to stop me from being baptized?"

Well, there was nothing at all to stop him. There was no reason not to bring this man into Jesus' life and grace. The chariot stopped, and right there, Philip baptized him. The Ethiopian went off in his chariot, and Philip continued preaching and teaching, building the body of Christ, the Church.

Based on Acts 6:1-7 and Acts 8:26-40.

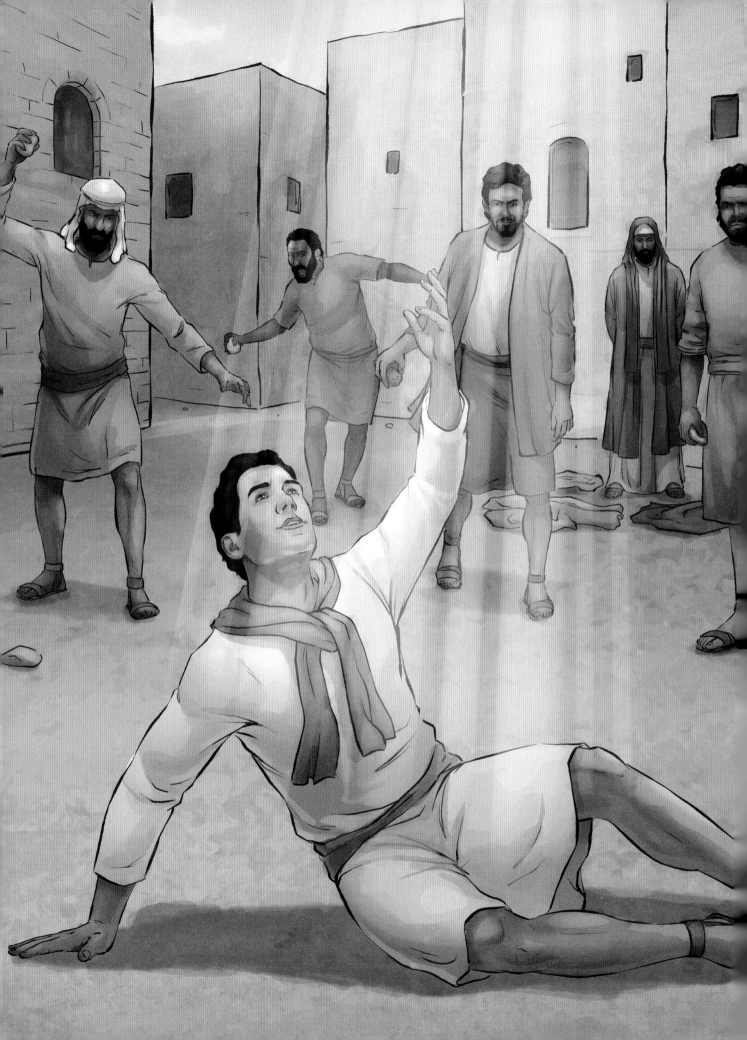

Stephen dies for his faith

Jesus had called his friends to follow him. So many times, in so many different ways, he had shown them what this road was like. It was a way of living in communion with him and receiving wisdom and strength by the Holy Spirit. It was a way of depending on God, of helping others and sharing God's mercy. To follow Jesus meant to put God first and build your house on his rock, not on sand that washes away with the wind and rain.

And, as he also told them many times, if they followed him there would be something else: a cross. There was no "might" or "could be" about it either. "If anyone wants to follow me," Jesus said, "let him deny himself and pick up his cross."

The apostles, around Jerusalem, were living in close communion with him in all those ways. They were following in Jesus' footsteps and shaping their lives to be like him. They were serving and were sharing his loving presence with each other and with all those they met.

Now it was time for the cross.

The religious leaders in Jerusalem who didn't like Jesus and had him put to death hadn't forgotten him. They weren't ignoring Jesus' followers either. And as the number of these followers grew, they were harder and harder to ignore.

One of the new deacons appointed by the apostles was named Stephen. Stephen was a young man and a wonderful preacher. In those days, Jesus' followers still considered themselves Jewish. Of course they were! Jesus had been Jewish, they were Jewish, and Jesus, they knew, was the Messiah sent by God for the Jewish people. How could they be anything but?

So in those early days, Jesus' followers tended to share the Good News mostly with other Jewish people. They would speak in and near the synagogues, explaining to anyone who would listen how Jesus was the fulfillment of all the prophet's words and, indeed, the Christ promised by God.

This is what the deacon Stephen was preaching one day near a certain synagogue in Jerusalem. Many of the people listening to him started arguing with him. They grew so angry and disturbed that they started to stir up trouble against him, spreading lies and

saying that he had spoken blasphemy. Well, this was a reason for Stephen to be taken to the religious court. He had begun his own way of the cross.

False witnesses were brought in who claimed that Stephen said Jesus would destroy the Temple and wanted his followers to change all the people's traditions.

The chief priest turned to Stephen. Was this true?

Now was the time. It was Stephen's chance to witness, to tell the leaders of the people every bit of the good news he could manage. And so he began at the very beginning, going all the way back to Abraham!

As Stephen told the story, he reminded those listening all about God's heart for his people through history. He retold the story of God's call to Abraham and his promise and covenant. He preached on Joseph's story, telling in detail how Joseph had been betrayed by his brothers and sold into slavery but had rescued the land through his dreams and his gifts. Moses was next. Stephen told the whole story of Moses, reminding all those gathered of how God's people had listened but also resisted, turned away, and even betrayed the Lord after he had freed them from slavery, putting their faith in a golden calf instead of God.

At every step of the way, Stephen reminded those gathered of how God was constantly offering love and mercy and even his very presence to his people and how often they had rejected him on that same journey from Abraham to the present moment.

It was, Stephen said, no different right now, at this moment. Nothing had changed.

"As your fathers did, so do you!" They receive the Law, he said, but don't keep it. And they reject the prophets! No wonder they had Jesus put to death.

These words, obviously, didn't please those listening to Stephen. He was comparing them to the worst of their ancestors. They were angry and enraged, but Stephen wasn't afraid at all. Standing there, he saw a vision—and he told them what he saw: Jesus, the one who had been crucified, standing at the right hand of God, the place of all God's authority and power. Jesus, crucified as a blasphemer, a criminal, just months before! At the right hand of God?

This they couldn't stand. The crowd rushed at Stephen and took him out of the city. They picked up stones. Not pebbles and sand, but heavy stones,

as heavy as they could manage. The crowd threw these stones at Stephen, striking him on every part of his body. This was the punishment for blasphemy. This was the punishment they thought Stephen deserved.

Stephen had walked in Jesus' footsteps, and here, outside the walls of Jerusalem, he was still walking with him. Jesus, accused of blasphemy, had been raised on a Cross outside these walls and made to suffer and die. Stephen was being killed for sharing the same message. Stephen, like Jesus, prayed that the Lord would receive his spirit as he approached death. And like Jesus, looking at those whose hands were raised to take his life, he prayed for the Lord's mercy—for them.

"Lord, do not hold this sin against them."

As Stephen died, another young man stood nearby, watching. As people rushed to pick up stones to throw at Stephen, they tossed their cloaks to the ground, and this young man was in charge of keeping them safe. His name was Saul.

Based on Acts 6:8–7:60.

Saul, former enemy of Christians, converts

I am the Way, the Truth, and the Life.
That's what Jesus had told his friends at the Last Supper. He's our way to the life God wants for us with him forever in heaven. That way through him begins here on earth, through prayer and loving acts. So as the early Christians followed Jesus, dedicating themselves to prayer and helping others, they became known as just that: "the Way."

This Way—of following Jesus, the Messiah—was known and was growing throughout the land of Israel. But not everyone was pleased about this. Stephen's martyrdom didn't end those bad feelings. In fact, one of the people who was there when Stephen was stoned to death continued on his own way of trying to hurt Christians. That man was Saul.

Saul was from the city of Tarsus. He was Jewish but also a Roman citizen and had studied his Jewish faith deeply and carefully with important teachers. Like the religious leaders in Jerusalem, he believed that those who were following Jesus were wrong and must be stopped. He used what he knew to hurt and persecute followers of the Way whenever he could.

One day, Saul was traveling to Damascus, a great city north of Israel, to find and arrest Christians. He had letters from the Temple's high priest to the synagogue in Damascus, telling those leaders that he, Saul, had permission to bring any followers of Jesus to Jerusalem for punishment. Saul was serious.

Saul approached Damascus. There on the road, he was suddenly surrounded by a bright light. It flashed around him, so bright that Saul couldn't see anything and fell to the ground.

He couldn't see, but he could hear, and what he heard at that moment was a voice.

"Saul, Saul," the voice said to him, "why do you persecute me?"

"Who are you, Lord?" Saul called out into the light from his own darkness.

"I am Jesus," the voice responded, "whom you are persecuting." And then that voice of Jesus told him to rise and go into Damascus—and he would then be told what to do.

Saul wasn't alone that day. Others were traveling with him too. Astonished,

they heard the voice but didn't see anyone speaking. Saul stood up from the ground and opened his eyes. But even with his eyes open, he couldn't see a thing. He was blind! So his friends took him by the hand and led him, as the voice had told Saul to go, into Damascus.

While all this was happening, a man in Damascus named Ananias had a vision. The Lord came to him, too, and told him to go to a certain house on a certain street and ask for Saul from Tarsus and lay his hands on him in prayer. Ananias, though, was a Christian, and had heard all about Saul. He'd heard how Saul had treated Christians in Jerusalem and why he was coming to Damascus. Surely it would be dangerous to visit this man.

In the vision, the Lord assured Ananias that not only was it safe but what was happening was for a very special purpose. Saul, the great persecutor, was to become a great witness for Jesus—and even take the Good News not only to more of the Jewish people but to Gentiles, or pagans, as well!

So Ananias obeyed the Lord and went to find Saul. He was, of course, exactly where God had said he would be. For three days, Saul had been blind and had eaten nothing. Ananias told Saul who he was and why he'd come, and he did as the Lord had directed. He laid his hands on Saul in prayer—and just like that, something like scales fell from Saul's eyes. He could see again!

Saul could see more than the things in the room and on the street. He could also see the truth now. He'd heard Jesus speak, he'd been healed of his blindness, and he'd been led to this place. So now it was time to get back on the road—but on a new journey this time, one that began with baptism into the life of the one he'd been persecuting—Jesus, the Lord.

Saul had been enthusiastic and energetic in doing battle with Christians. He was just as enthusiastic and energetic now, as he spoke for Jesus. He began in the synagogues of Damascus, where everyone who heard him was amazed—wasn't this the man who had brought harm to those who proclaimed Jesus' name? And now he was preaching that this same Jesus is the Son of God? It was confusing and hard to understand. It angered some so much that they tried to hurt Saul.

It was time to move on, but the Jewish leaders were guarding the city gate day and night. How could Saul escape? In a basket, which the disciples lowered over the walls of Damascus! And so Saul headed to Jerusalem.

If those in Damascus were confused by the change in Saul, it was even harder for the Christians in Jerusalem to understand. He returned to the city where Jesus had been crucified and had risen, where the Way had been planted and first taken root, and where not too long before, Saul had stood guard over the cloaks of those stoning Stephen.

Of course they were doubtful about Saul! Of course they were frightened! They found it very hard to believe that this man, of all people, had come to believe in Jesus and wasn't actually there to hurt them.

But one of the apostles—Barnabas—stood up for Saul. He brought him to the apostles and told his story and witnessed to what Jesus had said to him on the road to Damascus. He told them how, ever since, he had been boldly preaching the Good News.

And so Saul was welcomed into the Way. He had met the Lord, and his life had been changed. He had a new life now, and like so many who'd been given new lives by God—people like Abram, Sarai, Jacob, and Simon—as a sign of that new life, he'd also have a new name: Paul.

Based on Acts 9:1-31.

Cornelius and friends become first baptized Gentiles

Cornelius was a Roman centurion living on the coast of the land of Israel, in a city called Caesarea. Peter, the fisherman and apostle, was staying in Joppa, south of Caesarea on the coast.

They didn't know each other. They'd never met. But through visions and dreams, God was about to bring them together for the sake of his kingdom.

To start with, Cornelius was certainly a Roman, and while he wasn't formally a member of the Jewish faith, he still had great respect for God's people. He might have eaten food that Jewish people were forbidden to eat, but he believed in the one true God, prayed, and practiced acts of charity. One night, an angel came to him in a vision.

"There's a man named Peter staying in a tanner's house in Joppa," he said. "Send men to Joppa and find him."

Cornelius was puzzled and even scared, but he knew it was the Lord who'd spoken to him, so he obeyed, and sent his men down the coast to Joppa.

The very next day, Peter went up to the rooftop of the house where he was staying to wait for food to be prepared and to pray—the roof would have been flat and a nice place to be in the sun and fresh air. Deep in prayer, it was Peter's turn to enter into the heart of God. As he prayed, he saw what looked like a great sheet drop down from the heavens. It was such a huge sheet, it covered the whole world. In the sheet were all kinds of animals, reptiles, and birds. A voice came to Peter, there on the roof, as he waited for his dinner: "Rise, Peter; kill and eat."

Peter looked at the sheet and saw all those animals. There were many of them he wasn't allowed to eat because they were forbidden by the Law of Moses: pork, shellfish like shrimp, and certain kinds of birds. He didn't want to disobey the Law! "No, Lord," he said. "I've never eaten anything unclean in my whole life!" The voice answered him: "What God has cleansed, you must not call common."

Three times the sheet was lowered, and then—it was gone.

As Peter was seeing all this in his prayer, trying to understand what it could mean, visitors arrived down at the gate of the house. They were Cornelius' men, asking if Simon called Peter was staying there. Still praying, Peter understood from the Holy Spirit that three men were downstairs looking for him—and that he was simply to go with them. They'd been sent by God!

The men explained to Peter who had sent them: Cornelius, who was a Gentile, but God-fearing and very much respected by the Jewish community in Caesarea, had been told by an angel to send for Peter. And so Peter, along with a few others, joined the men, and the next day they all set out for Caesarea.

Cornelius welcomed them to his home—and he wasn't alone. His whole family was present, all Gentiles, gathered there to see Peter. But as Peter said to Cornelius, the Law which he observed was strict. Through the Law, God's people were set apart. They acted, dressed, and ate differently, not for their own sake, but to witness to the Lord, as he had commanded them from Moses' time. Because of this, Peter really wasn't supposed to share social times with Gentiles like Cornelius and his family. Why, he asked, had Cornelius invited him?

So Cornelius shared his experience with Peter. He told him of his prayer and the angel, and he told Peter how much he trusted the Lord. If all this had happened—if God had told him to find Peter, and they'd found Peter right where the angel had said—surely there was a reason. Cornelius invited Peter to speak to them.

And then Peter understood. He remembered his own vision. He looked around at the family and friends gathered there, the Gentiles who had welcomed him and were ready to listen. So he spoke:

"Truly I perceive that God shows no partiality," he said.

And then Peter told all those gathered in Cornelius' house about Jesus. He told the story from the beginning, telling of Jesus' baptism, his preaching, and his healing. Peter assured them that he'd seen all of this himself—he'd been a witness. Cornelius and his family were hearing about Jesus for the first time. He had been crucified, Peter told them, but on the third day he rose from the dead. Peter had seen him! Peter and the other apostles had shared meals with him! And Jesus had commanded them to go out and share this Good News, to testify that Jesus is Lord and that all who believe in him are forgiven of their sins!

It was a moment filled with the Holy Spirit, and in that moment the Jewish followers of Jesus who'd come with Peter from Joppa were amazed. They were surprised to see the Lord's Spirit working there in a new way, in the hearts of people they had been taught they shouldn't even share a meal with. Was there any reason not to find water and baptize everyone there who believed in Jesus? No!

Peter had preached the story of Jesus, the crucified and risen Lord, at Pentecost. There in Jerusalem he had shared this Good News with his fellow believers, with Jews. Today, the circle expanded. Today the Way, the Truth, and the Life was offered to all nations, as the prophets had foretold, as Peter told the story of Jesus there in the home of the Roman centurion named Cornelius.

Based on Acts 10.

Peter is freed from prison by an angel

After Stephen was martyred, some of Jesus' followers stayed in Jerusalem, but others left the city, taking the Good News to areas where people might be friendlier. They spread through the Roman Empire, north and south, east and west. One of the cities where they settled was Antioch, north of Galilee. Paul and Barnabas taught there for a time, and it was there that the followers of the Way were first called Christians.

But back in Jerusalem, there was trouble and suffering. The Romans were still in control of Israel, and they often used the leaders of the Jewish people to do their will. By this time, it was another Herod on that throne. Herod Agrippa was the grandson of the Herod who, after Jesus' birth, had ordered babies in Bethlehem killed to destroy the newborn king.

And he was the nephew of the Herod who had questioned Jesus at his trial.

This Herod turned his cruelty on the followers of Jesus. He persecuted some in Jerusalem, created the second Christian martyr—James the apostle, the brother of John—and finally turned on Peter, whom he had arrested and put into prison.

The followers of Jesus were praying for Peter. On the night they expected Herod to have him condemned, Peter was chained, sleeping between two soldiers in a cold, stone prison in Jerusalem. More soldiers guarded the prison door.

In the dark of night, an angel appeared in Peter's cell. Light shone all around, and the angel struck Peter in the side. It was time to wake up!

The chains fell from Peter's hands. The angel told Peter to get dressed, put his sandals on, wrap himself in a cloak, and follow him. Peter did. The angel led the way out of the prison, passing the first and second guard, and as Peter made his way away from the soldiers and through the prison, he couldn't be sure what was happening. He didn't know if he was really escaping or simply dreaming.

They left the prison and went through the gate to the city, and the angel disappeared. Now Peter was wide awake. Yes, this was real. Yes, that was an angel. And yes, he was free!

Through the streets of the city, Peter made his way to the place where he knew many of his friends would be staying and waiting: the house of a woman named Mary, who was the mother of a Christian named John Mark.

The door, of course, was closed and locked tight, because so many of Jesus' followers were being arrested and persecuted. Peter knocked on the door.

A young woman named Rhoda came to the door. She didn't open it, but she heard Peter's voice—and she was so happy, she ran back to tell all the others in the house that Peter was outside.

And so Peter waited outside and knocked again, knocked and waited—in the street, in the night—for someone to realize it was him and let him come in. Inside, they were confused. The last they heard, Peter had been arrested and was chained in prison, behind heavy stone walls and massive doors. And now Rhoda was saying he was right here, at their door?

"You're crazy!" they told her.

"No," she said. "I know it's Peter."
"Well," the people answered, "perhaps it's an angel." Even that would be more believable than to think it was Peter.

Finally, someone opened the door— and they saw that he was really there! Yes, it was Peter, and they listened as he told them how the Lord had worked through an angel to set him free and send him back to them.

Jesus called people from all walks of life to follow him. He preached and taught, he healed, he shared the Father's welcome and mercy, and he brought women and men, boys and girls into communion with him. After Jesus'

ascension into heaven, the community grew deeper and wider. New friends of Jesus were baptized. They shared in his Body and Blood in the Eucharistic meal. They became his body—the body of Christ that we call his Church.

As Jesus did during his life on earth, the members of his body, the Church, loved and served and shared mercy and Good News. They also suffered. But like Peter, the friends of Jesus who are his body can always find hope, even in the suffering, sometimes in the most surprising and unexpected ways.

Based on Acts 12:1-17.

Paul travels the world and survives a shipwreck

The Roman Empire was vast.
The city of Rome was, of course, the center of this great earthly power. But the Romans took their culture all across northern Africa, east to Spain, and north all the way to England. They built good roads and used fast ships to trade goods and information and news. And now the followers of Jesus followed those roads and routes to spread the best news of all, the Good News about Jesus the Lord!

It was along these roads and on these seas that Paul traveled. Joined by companions, earning his living as a maker of tents, he made his way to the lands of Asia Minor, which we now call Turkey. Then he traveled east to Greece and finally to Rome itself.

Paul made three major missionary journeys and had different adventures on each. In most places, he followed the same pattern of preaching and teaching. When he came to a new town, he'd go to the synagogue first. This was the main place of prayer for Jewish people who lived outside of Jerusalem and couldn't worship at the Temple.

Here they listened to readings from the Bible and studied God's Word.

Along with everyone else in the synagogue, Paul and his friends would listen to readings from the Law and the Prophets. Then Paul would take his turn to speak. He'd be talking to people who already understood that there was one God, not many, and that God had acted through the history of the Jewish people from Abraham through the prophets. He'd talk to people who were expecting God to send them a Messiah, a Savior—and now Paul could tell them that their prayers had been answered. The promised one had come. He had been crucified, died, and rose from the dead, and now he reigned as Lord. His name was Jesus!

Paul didn't meet people just in the synagogues, though. He met them on the road, in the public places where communities gathered, and even by the riverside. This is what happened near the city of Philippi, in an area called Macedonia, north of Greece.

How had Paul been led to this place? As so often happened, he came there by being open to God's prompting, no matter how it came. This time it had come to Paul in a dream. He thought he was to go to preach in Asia Minor, or Turkey, but he wasn't able to get there, and in the night, in a vision, he saw a man from Macedonia begging him to come there. It was clear to Paul that this is what the Lord wanted.

This was on Paul's second missionary journey, and there in Philippi, outside the city gates by the river, was a spot where people often gathered to pray. Paul and his companion met and spoke with those who had come. They spoke about Jesus and shared the Good News. One of the people there was named Lydia, a merchant who traded in purple cloth. Listening to Paul, she came to believe in Jesus, and there she and her household were baptized and welcomed into the life of the body of Christ.

In Philippi, Paul and his friend Silas were troubled by a slave girl. This poor girl was possessed by a demon, which gave her the power to tell the future. Her owners made money from this. With the demon inside her, the slave girl followed Paul and Silas around the town, shouting and drawing attention to them. This wasn't how Paul wanted to be noticed. He spoke in the name of Jesus to the demon, which immediately left the girl—and left her owners without the money it was making for them, too. This angered them, and they decided to get Paul and Silas into trouble.

So these men went to the authorities and reported Paul and Silas. As others had done before—with Stephen, with Peter, and of course with Jesus himself—the men stirred up trouble by claiming that Jesus' followers were troublemakers. They said Paul and Silas were telling people not to obey Roman authority—so of course Paul and Silas were thrown in prison.

Paul and Silas knew that no matter where they were, God was with them, and no matter what was happening, God should still be praised. So they spent the evening praying and singing psalms, and all the prisoners heard them.

As they were praying, the ground shook. The earthquake was so strong that the prisoners' chains were loosed, and they prepared to escape. When the jailer saw this, he was afraid, for if they escaped, he would be in very big trouble. And so, thinking that this was the end for him too, he took out his sword, not to hurt anyone else but to kill himself.

Paul stopped him. He cried out to let the jailer know that the prisoners were still there. The jailer, who had heard the men praying and singing all night and had felt the earth shake under his feet, could hardly believe it. He asked them, "What must I do to be saved?"

Paul told him right then and there. He told him about Jesus and said, "Believe in the Lord Jesus and you will be saved, you and your household." So that very night, the man who had guarded Paul and Silas in prison took them to his own home, where he washed their wounds. And then he and his family and everyone in his house were baptized. They were the ones set free that night, freed by Jesus from the prison of sin and death!

The next day, the magistrates released Paul and Silas but told them to leave Philippi right away. So they said goodbye to all the Christians there and continued on their way.

On one of Paul's journeys, the ship he was on was caught in a violent storm. It was badly damaged, but Paul assured the others on board, all 276 of them, that no one would come to harm. Only the ship would be lost. And that is what happened. The ship ran aground near the island of Malta, and everyone made it safely to shore. They stayed there for three months, preaching and healing as Jesus had done. The people were kind, and many became Christians.

Based on Acts 13:1–14:28 (first journey), 15:36–18:22 (second journey), and 18:23–21:16 (third journey).

The Church takes shape

In so many ways,

Jesus' teachings are so clear. They're not easy, but they are direct. *Blessed are the poor. Go and sin no more. Be merciful as your heavenly Father is merciful. I am the Way, the Truth, and the Life. I am the Bread of Life.*

And so the twelve apostles and Paul and his companions preached and spread this Good News. People were baptized and shared their goods with the poor, and they came together to celebrate the Eucharist. They tried to live lives of deeper mercy and goodness.

Most of these people came from a Jewish background and still thought of themselves as Jewish, and they still observed the Law of Moses. They stayed away from certain foods and even continued to pray in the Temple and in synagogues. This made sense to them. They understood that Jesus was the Messiah God's people had been waiting for. He was, as he said, fulfilling the Law, not replacing it.

But soon enough, it wasn't just Jewish people who were turning to Jesus. As Christians moved beyond Jerusalem, they shared the Good News with people from all backgrounds. What about them? If a Gentile accepted Jesus as Lord and wanted to be baptized and a part of the body of Christ, would that person be Jewish, too? Would they be expected to observe all the Jewish laws? Or would living by Jesus' direct words be enough?

Even after Peter's vision and the baptism of Cornelius and his household, this problem wasn't solved. For in Antioch, some Christian teachers were telling the new Gentile believers that they must observe the Law in every detail. Paul and Barnabas disagreed. Returning to Jerusalem, they found more of the same. Christian teachers were claiming that for anyone to be a Christian, that person had to be Jewish as well and observe the Law. This problem wasn't going to just go away. They had to face it.

The apostles and other leaders gathered in Jerusalem. They shared their ideas and experiences. They debated. They disagreed. After listening to all the points of view and every side, Peter stood up to speak—Peter, who'd had the vision of the clean and unclean animals, who had baptized Cornelius' Gentile household. It was Peter who stood up now before this first Church council, the Council of Jerusalem, and spoke on behalf of the Gentiles who had come to love Jesus.

He'd seen the Holy Spirit come into the lives of Gentiles, just as the Spirit had moved those who came from a Jewish background. God's Spirit hadn't put up walls. God's Spirit hadn't made any distinction between the Gentiles and the Jews—the Holy Spirit had been poured out into the hearts of all, from every background.

Peter said the question was, Who were they, mere human beings, to put up walls? Who were they to put those differences in stone? Who were they, when God's people weren't perfect in observing the Law of Moses themselves anyway? It was through God's grace that all of them, Jew and non-Jew, were saved.

As the group quietly thought about Peter's words, Paul rose to speak along with Barnabas, who had traveled with him. Together, they too described the many signs and wonders they had seen God working among the Gentiles.

Then James, the leader of the Christians in Jerusalem, stood up. He had taken it all in—not only what Peter, Paul, and Barnabas said, but what the prophets before them had revealed about what God would do in the fullness of time. He reminded them of what Amos, Jeremiah, and Isaiah had all foretold: a time when God would rebuild and restore his creation—with all people gathered to him. All people, from all over the world.

Therefore, James said, it was clear to him that they should put as few obstacles up as they could. And in a letter that they sent out to all the Gentile believers, the leaders of the Church shared the news. Led by the Holy Spirit, praying, discussing, and listening, they had come to a deeper understanding together. They had heard what great faith was growing among the Gentiles, and they didn't want to put up any barriers.

So, they said, someone from a Gentile background who had come to believe in Jesus and was baptized would simply be asked to observe some very basic parts of the Law. When it came to food, Gentiles were asked to avoid just a few things, like not eating food that had been offered to idols or the meat of animals that had been strangled. There were reasons for those.

First, meat from animal sacrifices to the pagan gods was regularly sold in the markets and used for ordinary food. It made sense to stay away from this kind of food, since it joined you to pagan worship. Second, when it came to meat, God had instructed the people through the Law how to kill animals for their food in merciful, painless ways—and strangling wasn't one of them. So any believer should stay away from this type of cruelty.

Believers should also, the letter said, treat their own bodies and their families in the way that God had commanded, for those actions of respect and care reflected the gifts of love and life that God gave Adam and Eve at Creation.

God had created the world, and every human being in his own image. He had called his people to bring wholeness back into the world. Jesus, the "Word made flesh," had come to dwell in that creation, bringing all people back into communion with God, free from sin and death. God's work to bring all of creation back to him was unfolding. Led by the Spirit, the body of Christ on earth was listening, learning, and growing stronger, breaking down walls so that all peoples, as the prophet Isaiah had foretold, would stream to his holy mountain and share in his feast forever!

Based on Acts 15.

The apostle John shares a vision of hope

Many years passed.

The apostles spread out through the known world. They preached the Good News, baptized thousands, and formed new Christian communities wherever they went, which was sometimes very far! Matthew traveled to Ethiopia in Africa, and Thomas went all the way to India!

They were traveling throughout the world in Jesus' footsteps—all the way to the Cross. For they would die as martyrs. Even Paul was beheaded in Rome, where Peter too died, crucified upside down.

By the end of the century, John, one of the Twelve, had not suffered a violent death, but he also wasn't free to do as he pleased. For John was in a prison of sorts. He had been sent into exile on a Greek island called Patmos.

John looked back. So much time had passed, and such a great distance had been traveled. It had all begun with a man walking by a lake, who invited some fishermen to follow him. And now, every day, lives were changed. Women and men, boys and girls were brought closer to the Lord, their sins forgiven and the gates of eternal life opened up to them—all over the world!

But two things hadn't changed and never would. One was the Good News of God's kingdom brought to earth and fulfilled in Jesus Christ. The other was the battle against that Good News.

Jesus told those who followed him to prepare for suffering and accept it. Why? Because the darkness remains, and the darkness will keep fighting God's light as it had from the beginning, when Satan first tempted Eve. This temptation and suffering would come into the life of every follower of Jesus and every Christian community, great or small.

But Jesus gave his apostles hope when he allowed them to see him transfigured right before his passion. And now God gave his children hope through John, living alone on Patmos, waiting for the Lord.

God often came to his children in visions and dreams, as he did now with John on Patmos. He showed John how to look at life on earth and see what was truly happening. John shared this vision of hope and trust with all the Church through a letter—a letter to seven churches in Asia, or what we now call Turkey.

We can read John's letter in Revelation, the last book of the Bible. It begins with a vision of Jesus. John heard a voice like a trumpet that told him to write what he was about to see. John turned to see who was speaking to him, and he saw, standing among seven golden lampstands … Jesus. Jesus was clothed in a long robe with a golden sash, and everything about him was white and flaming like fire, his voice flowing deeply and surely like strong waters, and his face shining like the sun.

John, struck with fear and awe, fell at Jesus' feet. And as he did so, the Lord laid his right hand upon him and told him not to be afraid.

"I am the first and the last," he said. "I am the living one. I died, and now I am alive forever. Write what you see!"

And so Jesus told John what to write in letters to the seven churches. We live on earth, where nothing is perfect. So all of these churches had problems. All had reasons to repent, grow, and change.

Some had grown wealthy and had forgotten how important it is to depend on God alone for happiness. Others were becoming too relaxed and were mixing with pagans. Still others were trying to keep their faith in Jesus but were losing heart because of persecution.

The letter to the church in Laodicea is like this. It begins, as all the letters do, addressed to the angel, or bishop, of the community. Then Jesus describes himself as the great Amen, the true witness, and the beginning of God's creation.

Laodicea was a town that produced fabrics and grew wealthy because of this industry. But as Jesus had said to his disciples, it is harder for a wealthy man to gain eternal life than it is for a camel to get through the eye of a needle. When we have all we need for our physical lives on earth, it can be hard to remember how much we need God. We can forget that none of the nice things that surround us will save us. In the end only the Lord forgives us, saves us, and gives us eternal life.

The Laodiceans had forgotten this. They were not turning their backs on the Lord completely, but they were "lukewarm, and neither cold nor hot." What does it mean to be lukewarm? It means you may not be working against someone, but you're not working for them either. And this is what the Christians of Laodicea were like. Jesus told them that while they said they needed nothing, the truth was that they had nothing. What should they do? They should seek the riches that only Jesus can give.

"Behold," Jesus says to the Christians of Laodicea, "I stand at the door and knock; if anyone hears my voice and opens the door, I will come in to him and eat with him, and he with me."

Jesus said that the journey to eternal life will be hard. We'll have to sacrifice, we'll have to be willing to change, and we'll have to turn away from many of the fun things that the world offers. Others won't like what we're doing. They'll mock us or try to stop us through insults, bad comments, or even threats. Jesus knew this. The apostles learned it. John, there on Patmos, was living it.

Our earthly way, this way of suffering, isn't the end. Jesus calls us to trust him and gives us hope as he walks among us, risen and whole. This is what he shares with us through John's Revelation: a vision of hope that trusts in him and holds firm. He promises that the darkness will be overcome. Our end is not pain but joy with him forever.

Based on the book of Revelation.

The Temple in Jerusalem is destroyed

The Temple in Jerusalem
stood with its strong walls, candles
burning, priests praying, and animals
sacrificed to the Lord. The Ark of the
Covenant was long gone, lost in the fogs of
destruction and captivity, but the Temple
still stood, a sign of God's presence.

King Solomon had overseen the building
of the first temple. Lined with precious
gold and cedar, it was a sign of the glory
of God and the wealth of Israel, too. But
the earthly glory was laid low by the
Babylonians, who leveled the Temple
when they conquered God's people.

But God's people returned, straggling
back to the Promised Land, led by
Zerubbabel, Ezra, and Nehemiah, to
rebuild their lives and the Temple as
well. Again it stood tall. Perhaps it was
not as elaborate and as rich as Solomon's
temple, but it too was beautiful, high
on the hill in Zion, where the people
worshipped the mighty, merciful God
who had saved and forgiven his children
over and over again through the years.

God's people were no longer
independent. They had suffered

under the Greeks and now, for decades, under the Roman Empire. But at least the Temple still stood. At least sacrifice was still offered there, smoke rising from Zion to the Lord, pleasing to his sight.

One day, Jesus was walking from the Temple in Jerusalem. He remarked to his friends, "Do you see these great buildings? There will not be left here one stone upon another that will not be thrown down."

Another time, Jesus simply wept. He looked over all of Jerusalem, including the Temple, and told his disciples that enemies would surround the city one day and dash everything to the ground. Not one stone would be left standing.

Time passed. Jesus died and rose and ascended into heaven. The Holy Spirit came upon the apostles, and the Church was born. The body of Christ grew, spreading throughout the world.

And then one terrible year, what Jesus had foretold came to pass.

By the year 66 AD, some of the Jewish people living in Jerusalem had had enough of Roman rule. They rebelled and fought hard for years. Vespasian was the Roman general who fought the Jewish rebels at first, but in 69, he was made emperor. He returned to Rome, and his son Titus took over the battle. Titus was determined. He would take Jerusalem.

In those days, it was common for armies to weaken a town or city by laying siege to it. That meant they would block all comings and goings through the city walls and starve the people inside until they died or surrendered. So Titus laid siege to Jerusalem, and finally, after months, the Romans were able to enter the city.

It is said that Titus didn't want to destroy the Temple, but in the end the Temple burned. Maybe a Roman soldier started the fire, or maybe it started in the confusion of battle. All that mattered to the Jewish people was that the Temple was destroyed, all except one wall, which still stands today. The worship God called for in the Old Covenant—the priesthood of the Levite tribe and the animal sacrifice—was no more.

But what else had Jesus said?

"Destroy this temple and in three days, I will raise it up again."

What else?

"This is the New Covenant in my blood."

The Lord drew his people close to him through the Old Covenant, through the Law of Moses and worship in the Temple. The people learned what it meant to be created in God's image and to be shaped and formed by God to live that out on earth. They honored God through worship and sacrifice, giving him their firstfruits in gratitude. They learned that God's mercy is, indeed, poured out for them and that he will always forgive.

And in Jesus, that Good News is showered on the whole world, to every person. As the prophet Jeremiah foretold, in Jesus the law and covenant of God's love and care are written no longer on stone like the tablets of the Ten Commandments but on our living hearts. God's mercy breaks through walls and is poured out into those hearts. We have always known, since the Garden of Eden, that we needed a Savior. Through the Old Covenant, God led his people on the journey to him, waiting for the Messiah. And at the manger in Bethlehem and at the Cross and the empty tomb in Jerusalem, we found him.

The Temple made of stones, built by human hands, was gone, but the temple of Jesus' body embraces the world as his Church. No more animal blood is shed for the sake of a covenant, because Jesus shed his own blood for us. In the New Covenant of his blood, human beings are brought back into the heart of the God who created them, forgiven and reconciled forever.

The Temple fell, but that holy temple of the body of Christ has risen, with him as its cornerstone and you and me as its living stones.

"And he came and preached peace
to you who were far off and peace to
those who were near;
for through him we both have access
in one Spirit to the Father.
So then you are no longer
strangers and sojourners,
but you are fellow citizens with the saints
and members of the household of God,
built upon the foundation of the
apostles and prophets, Christ Jesus
himself being the cornerstone,
in whom the whole structure is
joined together and grows into a
holy temple in the Lord;
in whom you also are built into it
for a dwelling place of God in the Spirit"
(Ephesians 2:17-22).

*Jesus' prophecies appear
in Matthew 24, Mark 13:2,
and Luke 19:41-44.*

Christians await Jesus' second coming

This world had a beginning.
The Bible tells us about that beginning: in God's love. The world began because God wanted it to be here. Through his word, God created the whole universe, and it was good—and that includes you!

This world will also have an end. The Bible tells this story, too. The beginning of the world is told in Genesis, the first book of the Bible, and it's in the last book, Revelation, that we read what will happen at the end.

In between, God's creation and every person created to live in it has been on an adventure. It's been an adventure of ups and downs, of steps forward and backward, of great tragedy and disappointment. But every step of the way, it's also been an adventure about joy, beauty, truth, and love. It's been an adventure led by good news: the good news that we're here because God loves us, and we're saved because God loves us and won't give up on us.

This is the good news God builds into us in our creation. It's the news that we forget and even turn away from, as our first parents did back in Genesis. It's the news that Jesus shared with us again and again when he walked on the earth.

It's the news his body on earth, the Church, shares with the whole world.

And it's the news that makes us eager for Jesus' return.

When will this happen? How will we know? And what will happen then?

"You do not know the day or the hour."

That's what Jesus told his friends. He spoke to them many times of what lies ahead at the end of this great adventure on earth, but he always warned that for us, human beings so much smaller than God, a great mystery lies at the heart of it.

Yes, the time will come, he said. He will return, and he will come back into the world in a special way, to judge. It will be like what a farmer does when he separates the good parts of grain from the bad or when he pulls weeds out of his field. It will be a time when Jesus asks all people how they've used the gifts of life and love the Creator gave them.

Did they feed Jesus when they met him, hungry? Did they visit him in prison? Did they clothe him when they met him naked or give him water when he was thirsty? Those on his right will be those who saw him in people in need, and those on his left, cast away, will be those who refused to share their gifts, passing the suffering by.

Yes, that time will come, Jesus told his friends. That time of judgment will be

our moment to see not only how much we matter to God but how much our choices matter, too.

And when will that time come? Jesus said there will be signs of his coming, but we won't ever be able to say for sure when it will be—though plenty of people will try to make you believe that they know.

When we know something's going to happen, but we're not sure when, we know what to do next: get ready. We get prepared.

Jesus talked about this, too. He told parables about women and men who work in the fields, attendants waiting for the bridegroom at a wedding, or servants waiting for their master to return. Some of them are alert and awake and can welcome the bridegroom or the master back home—and some are asleep and miss him.

This Second Coming is an end, in one way. But because God is good and merciful and his love is eternal, it's also a beginning. For in the midst of all this mystery of when and how, Jesus shows us something very clearly: his empty tomb and himself, risen, holding out his hands to us. He gives us a glimpse, just as he gave that glimpse to Peter, James, and John when he was transfigured before their eyes. He gives us a glimpse of both the end of one road and the beginning of God's new creation through what he revealed to John and what John shared with us in that last book, the book called Revelation.

God created a beautiful world, giving us all that we need for happiness, but through sin, we brought ugliness and death into that world. Through John's vision, the Lord shows us that no matter how great our suffering or how sad the world seems, he is, indeed, returning to restore it. Jesus, through his passion, death, and resurrection, has reconciled all of creation, and in time, that creation will be restored, like a new Garden of Eden, to him. Those who have said yes to the Lord on this earthly adventure and have chosen the best ways they could to use their gifts to help will be right there with him.

And John saw this. He saw a new heaven and a new earth, a new holy city. In that place, filled with light, God will dwell with his people forever and will wipe away every tear. There will be no more death, no more crying or sadness or pain for those who have loved the Lord.

John saw a New Jerusalem, but there was no temple, because Jesus, the Lamb of God, was himself the temple. There was no sun, no moon or stars to give light, because it was filled with the glory of God—and what other light do we need?

The gift that the Lord gave John was a vision of beauty and richness. The New Jerusalem is what Eden was meant to be. It glistens. It flows with life-giving waters and is nourished by the Tree of Life. It is filled with the sounds of joy and praise.

The journey has been hard, and the adventure has been challenging and strange, exciting and mysterious. But God has never left his people to wander alone. He pushed, he nudged, he whispered, he led, he disciplined, and he forgave. Again and again he forgave, until finally, he gave his own Body and Blood. And at last, heaven and earth were reconciled.

Genesis to Revelation tells the story of that great adventure, from beginning to end. But the end is not yet, and it is really not the end at all, for God's life is an adventure of love that never ends. God's love is poured out in creation, from the bigness of the universe to each tiny beating human heart. That love, in him, is all and everything. In him is the beginning, and in him is the end.

"I am the Alpha and the Omega, the first and the last, the beginning and the end …
Come, Lord Jesus!"
(Revelation 22:13, 20)

Based on Matthew 24:36-51, Mark 13:32-37 and 14:62, John 3:16, Romans 2:6-11, 2 Timothy 4:1, and Revelation 21:1-8.